The St. Lawrence

The St. Lawrence

Mia and Klaus

Text by Pierre Perrault

Translated by Diana Lesley Webb

Québec ▪▪

Libre Expression

Art Global

This book was published with the assistance of the Quebec Government: Project Saint-Laurent of the department of the Executive Council and la Direction générale des publications gouvernementales du ministère des Communications.

We thank the Commissariat général aux célébrations 1534-1984 for assisting the photographers who created this book.

We wish to thank the Cultural Affairs branch of the federal Department of Communications for assisting with the publication of this book.

The authors wish to thank Air Canada, Québecair and Air France for their collaboration.

Toutes isles, Éditions Fides
© Pierre Perrault
Distribution: l'Hexagone

© Éditions Libre Expression/Art Global, 1984

Legal deposit:
1st trimester 1984

ISBN 2-89111-180-X

For my Father
who taught me the sea and the stars...
Klaus

And for Gilbert
who beyond the stars showed us other paths...
Mia

Whom shall we follow? The seagull? The eager navigator? The sailing boats? How shall we approach the Saint-Laurent, how can we capture its complexity? Where in the sea will we find it hiding, from what point in history can we call it forth, where find its original traces, the indiscernible beginnings?

We decided to start our voyage from the estuary of the Saint-Laurent and follow the wake left by Jacques Cartier's ship when he first mapped the seapassage. Entering was simple — but the voyage out? And how to sail away after that? For the river held us captive an entire year, our hearts enchanted. The river has changed our lives and we will never be the same again after these four serene seasons: now part of us will always belong to the sea, the ships, the rock-bound-coast.

All day long the water moved beneath us and this undulating rythm penetrated our very being as if the waves dwelt within us, never ceasing to surge, and even in the night we could not suppress them: they followed us into our very dreams, lulling us to sleep.

From the open sea, to the gulf, to the river and onwards, passing the shorepoints where other major rivers join the Saint-Laurent, we sailed upstream following the sea passage inland. We observed its many aspects as every different day passed, and at every hour of the day. We saw its many moods and colours: green at noontime like swaying grass on a prairie rose beneath the setting sun, silver under the moonlight sky, and as smooth as silk and flecked with gold in the dawn and overwhelming light of morning. And we saw, also, more violent colours, reddish black at dawn as harbouring dark designs.

There were nights, too, when the gulf rebelled in sudden rage hurling itself at the isles, determined perhaps to drown them as wave after wave crashed on the riverbanks in an ever more violent onslaught, dragging the red earth out to sea like streaks of blood in the churning white foam.

Gulf that is still a sea, gulf that is already a river as the salt water flows inland — we also listened to its many sounds, this music of water and wind risen from the fathoms below or following us from the high seas, and the plaintive groan of water on the reefs where so many ships and so many lives had been lost. Both music and song these sounds, the wail of wind and water like words of some strange language that can nevertheless be understood, the cries of drowning men, the haunting voices of sirens, calling and calling...

Sometimes surveying the panorama from an airplane we traced the river's capricious path. One day, as the clouds opened suddenly before us, we saw a coastline of cliffs below us, red and rugged, massive and multiform as they rose in the sky.

The plane, leaning on one wing as it flew, revealed a bird's-eye view of a landscape like a necklace of rocks mounted on golden clasps. And this gold was the fine sand of the dunes on the group of islands called "les îles de la Madeleine", adrift in the sea and forming a chain of nearly one hundred kilometres of uninterrupted beauty... Cliffs suspended dangerously over the sea, rounded hills inexplicably bulging the earth's surface, silent springs where wild and magical blue herons flee at the slightest sound, the slightest presence... Sandunes as far as the eye can see where terns swoop and swirl... Reefs... Crags of rock rising out of the sea adorned with white seabirds... Grottos where waves disappear leaving behind a sparkling fan of white foam... Island like some Paradise stranded on the outskirts of a forest of sea, "Beau à percer le coeur" as one Madelino poet said to me—a beauty that pierces the heart!

Flying over the North Shore, further than Sept Îsles, further than Rivière-au-Tonnerre, we saw also the vast country on shore. Forests, rivers, streams, brooks, rapids, marshlands, peat bogs. And at the foot of the cliffs, the river winding along like a ribbon of light in the dark green and brown hues of the landscape. Facing so much wild beauty, we could easily imagine times gone by when the first pioneers roamed these savage gardens of Eden.

Anticosti: rapids, torrents, rivers leaping from tier-of-rock to tier-of-rock descending like steps towards the sea. Discreet coves of rivers where stags and does followed by their fawns, newborn in the spring, come tranquilly to drink. Dense forests peopled with happy beasts that dwell in castles of forest shadows and under the rooftops of the leafy boughs of trees. An arch of silence where mankind whispers as in a temple... In the pure black sky of its nights, the island gathers a harvest of stars: nowhere else do they shine so brightly, like firewords as they change position and move closer towards the Earth in July.

On certain privileged nights the skies of Anticosti are lighted by the Aurora Borealis. These undulating patterns of light seem like huge cathedrals in the sky, like fountains and waterfalls of cascading light, wavering and swaying in the moving darkness of the sky, a thousand bright rays spreading out in all directions, making the night dance under translucid veils of rainbow colours. And then these huge blazing fires of the night sky are quenched by the blackness of infinite space, leaving Anticosti invisible in the darkness.

Sailing up from the gulf into the river, we noticed one day a monstrous ship looming towards us through the fog, circled by hundreds of seagulls. As we drew near, we saw its full outline and identified the massive rock of Percé. Across from this, Île Bonaventure. The cliffs here are a fortress haven for seabirds, and the baby gannets recently hatched were rolled-up in their down feathers like balls. On the green carpet of surrounding sea and the grassy border of the sheer cliffs, and even on the very face of the rock, thousands and thousands of seabirds live in harmony on this isle like an immense nest divided into the minute territories of each bird couple, black guillemots, cormorants, gannets, and above all the seagulls, of diverse size and variety known here mostly as "mouettes", "marmites" or "goélands". From May to September the sky above Île Bonaventure vibrates with the ceaseless spreading of wings.

Soon, along the periphery of the river, we would pass a shoreline dotted with beautiful names of places such as: Cap-Bon-Ami, Cap-des-Rosier, Anse-au-Griffon, l'Échouerie, Manche-d'Épée, Anse-Pleureuse, Ruisseau-à-Rebours, Cap-Chat, Trois-Pistoles, Cacouna, Rivière-du-Loup, Cap Tourmente. But in the meantime, we detoured to sail in exploration of the Saguenay, deep as the night of history and bordered by steep cliffs. It reminded us of a chapter in the Bible, "Book of Job", where the Lord says: *Or who shut up the sea with doors, when it brake forth, as if it had issued out of the womb?*
When I made the cloud the garment thereof, and thick darkness a swaddling band for it;
And brake up for it my decreed place, and set bars and doors;
And said, Hitherto shalt thou come, but no further: and here shall thy proud waves by stayed.

And these cliffs on each side of the river recalled these doors, and the fog recalled this swaddling band, and we were hence transported to the Sixth Day of Creation where the Lord had created the world and "... *saw that it was good.*" By nightfall we had reached the foot of Cap Trinité. The night poured into the river with all its stars, their reflections giving the impression that we were surrounded by a sky of stars both above and below us. And the stars with their light seemed also within us, and even more so than outside of us. Thus showing us that all is ONE.

On our return to the Saint-Laurent, entering the region known as "le bas du fleuve", we stopped to see the migrating wild geese. A hundred thousand pairs of wings beat the air as they flew overhead, ploughing furrows in the sky with delirious joy. Dazzled witnesses to this vision, we recalled the words of wisdom that exhort the joy one can take in each moment throughout life: *"Et qu'est-ce qu'une flamme, ô mes amis, si ce n'est le moment même, ce qu'il y a de fol et de joyeux et de formidable dans l'instant même?"*

This river that we have followed, seeking its traces in the Atlantic, and sailing from its initial salt waters and trembling waves to the place where, as perhaps God himself ordained, it would become a river, this river become ours by right of love, we are pleased to introduce you to this river, the Saint-Laurent...

Mia Matthes

Blanchon
My Friend the
White Whale

le lendemain au matin, fismes voille et appareillames pour passer oultre:

et eusmes congnoissance d'une sorte de poisson desquelz il n'est mémoire d'homme avoir veu ny ouy,

lesditz poissons sont aussi groz comme morhoux (marsouins), sans avoir aucun estocq

et sont assez faitz par le corps et teste de la façon d'un lévrier, aussi blancs comme neige, sans avoir aucune tache

et y en a moult grand nombre dedans ledict fleuve qui vivent entre la mer et l'eaue doulce: les gens du pays les nomment adhothuys.

Jacques Cartier

"A monster resembling a siren..."

Samuel Fallours, 1718

Far too vast for one man alone, the sea, here on a beach of rushes or there of slate, surges up to the very finger-tips of the mountain! How can I resist the sea that flows through my veins believing itself infinite?

I was gazing at the sea shaped by the shoreline where it cradles forever a dream without heed of the land. I was watching the sea at work, a force driven to deliver up precious stones and polish the agate pebbles! How can I believe in these undefined oceans which claim that sirens, their "sereines de mer", do not exist?

Time, unanchored, sailed in discovery of an island immemorial!

Waiting perhaps for the unforeseen, hoping for the unhoped-for, I gave silent moments their chance to speak, colours their stage for drama, music to every sound, like a man limited to exploring legend.

I could have contented myself with routes, the land-scape in the mind's eye, which invent detours, cut through valleys and lead always to that common graveyard where the generations lie at anchor. But what is to be done with a path that does not end at the head of the tides, and begins where it cannot end, and leads to whence nobody has finally nor ultimately returned.

Then, then, then... a white whale which was swimming in this narrow sea the villages had moored seemed to offer me a sign to take my astrolabe and measure the heaven's at his side, as if wanting to help me shake the dust from the portulans and fill them with new adventures.

I was complaining about the sea to which I had bound myself not with ease but with the difficulty of a poor soul used to living on the surface of things. The sea was too vast for the eyes of a man whose life had been spent pouring over books.

Blanchon—for that is the name I called him by so that he would hear me—said to me, "Have you never penetrated into the very interior of the sounds and silences and the thousand colours that are divided in the waters by the keels of ships?"

Then, then, then... I no longer hesitated. And I said, "Come, Blanchon, my friend!... Without bridle!... Without stirrup!... Without saddle!... On a daring ride!... Little matter our return and the twists of fate that lie ahead!... Let us depart without compass!... Nor astrolabe!... Nor road to follow!... On the back of a white white whale."

Because there's a river for us to discover—somewhere between the sea and the fresh water—where white whales have always tamed the shore and man. If it were not for the white whales' epic, what report would there be of the reefs?

A Rolling Stone...

I wanted to live without taking count! Without keeping track of the days, the nights, the distances, the regrets... A full moon night!

Of all the means of travel, you will say, why did you choose the most inclement?

By chance and by fate! And I will add for those who always want to know still more: Because the portulans of the ancients showed, along with their sirens and their monsters which swallowed up ships, always a drawing of a white whale or dolphin to represent discovery.

On the shores, the navigators have a saying, "Moon descending, tide rising, Cap Tourmente," and the wisdom it contains serves as a guide to sailing the defiant waters. I wanted to understand words such as these that invoke moon, sea and anguish. I wanted to live without regrets and without limits... A night of the open seas... Far from anchorage... A full moon night... To escape all doubts!

From that day on, the inhabitants of Escoumins and Anse aux Basques have told the sad story of a fisherman carried off on the white back of a runaway river. On beaches of slate and clay. In the night. In the moon. Without the slightest ulterior motive. Without the slightest regret. Abandoning the luxurious comfort of books to live the spoken word unadulterated. In every cove. As if gathering the most important fruits of wisdom.

"Blanc, blanc loup-marin..."
Quebec Folklore

I must tell you why I chose to call him Blanchon. He had no precise name, and words of a kind for species were of no help for establishing a personal friendship.

The Russians gave him the name Bélukha, and the French transcribed this as Béluga despite the fact that the latter word designates, in the Russian language, the sturgeon. The Eskimos, they had the word Killeluak, a beautiful but difficult word, strange and sounding a little like Russian. I was already, to tell you the truth, short of words and had much to say of such a river "qui vas si loing que jamais homme n'avoit esté jusques au bout qu'ils eussent ouy" ("that goes so far that never has a man been to its end").

Luckily a silence of such stature does not go without saying. And I listened to what was said on shore. And I heard that those who dwelled by this river and who were great hunters of this animal, call it a porpoise, or "marsouin", and the English say "white whale" though in fact it is a member of the dolphin family. Was I on the right track, then? That of a spoken word that had travelled far and wide.

Yes indeed the Indians had repeated the word "Adho-thuys" to Jacques Cartier to designate the huge white carcases the seagulls were attacking which lay on the beds of seaweed, slate and pebbles of the astonishing "ysle ès Couldres" about which he tells us, in 1534, that "là se faiet, par ceulx du pays, grande pescherye des dicts adhothuys" (there much fishing of the "adhothuys" is carried on by those of this country).

Yes indeed the scholarly argue among themselves with words fit for cookery books and perfectly unserviceable on a voyage: delphinapterus leucas!

Blanchon says, "I am an animal unknown to many. And I do not speak latin."

Why did I choose a word that comes from the common language and so has been called vulgar? Because those words put all the others to shame!

At Ouelle River, the young whales are called "veau" (calf) or "gris" (gray one) or else "blafard" (pallid one) because they are as yet not completely white and since they are born the gray hue of an October day.

At Escoumins and near the shores of the Outardes river and the Manicougan river, the hunters call them instead "bleuvet" (bluish one) or "blanchon" (white one) according to the colour and that is a matter of age since the whales change from their natal gray to blue and from blue to white as they grow, and only to white after the three years they spend out on the high seas.

From among all these words mostly abandoned today, I chose the name Blanchon because my friend appeared to be closest to that white of the white white whales. I chose Blanchon because such a river claims possession of the sea and its fishes, and how can we remain silent though books have resisted such names for fifteen generations of man, of land, and of sea.

"Trouver le levant par le nort ou le su..."
Champlain

I was, for a longtime, limited to the semblance of a voyage. But neither can one tell all of what happens.

The sea, faithful to the past, surged again and again on the shore, from moon to moon ever sifting through its treasure coffers sparkling brimful with tiny fishes —capelins, smelt, and loach—as if it were itself some sunken galleon from the Caribeean, its hold ripped open, pouring forth pieces of gold and silver.

Blanchon, plunging with open jaws into this May moon shining on the reefs deserted by the tide at Pointe aux Alouettes, says to me "We are worth millions."

In this area the river can be mistaken for some smaller river where churches reflected in the water stand calmly on their spires. And yet twice a day these images are buried by the clay ooze left in the wake of the tide. And yet people of villages here, when they talk of harvests and sunshine and chance, ask themselves always what the sea will make of it, as they already know the influence of the moon that induces nature's fecundity.

And yet I have but one life, that formed of white sands and some seaweed, as mine to exchange for my desires of a full moon and the open seas. A life that was still entangled in books and had never left schools to fish for cod at open sea. A life still buried in the bronze of beaches and which knew nothing of the ocean but the empty concave hollow of seashells.

Blanchon, having guessed my false pretexts, felt disinterest for all these riches, and one night at that precise moment when the moon can mistake a dolphin for a ship and when a white whale that navigates the uncertain oceans can lose his bearings and be in the wrong epoch or guess the wrong instinct, we departed on our quest for an unknown river.

Blanchon said only, "To love the sea it is not enough to have riches."

And to escape complacency, we abandoned the beautiful polar herds which slept adrift in a sea of silver and moonlight worth millions.

Out on the Open Sea

Once we had avoided several of the fish traps called "fascines" that are familiar sights in the waters around Île aux Coudres where the moon unloads its cargo of fresh fish with the tide, Blanchon said to me, "Sleep. I will keep watch."

Not wanting to miss any part of this adventure story, I told him my secret. "I must keep watch on a star for the sake of love."

Blanchon smiled at the moon and then headed out in the direction of the sun, all the better to reach morning, there where the world has escaped from tragedy but not without effort.

Night, with all its stars, was not as vast as my enchantment. Believing myself alone on these waters, I counted the waves as if I were gathering fruit fallen from a tree in the foolish hope of keeping each one as a souvenir.

Music like that of an accordion flowed from a little green star that was on our left, just above the horizon, and spread across the water like an oil, as if to calm the sea and perhaps lull it to sleep.

Blanchon swam towards the green undulating star to greet a "goelette" (a topsail schooner) which was named like a village. We could hear the crew singing the tune "Belle Embarquez" to the accompaniment of the motor's throbbing. And in this digression, my conversation came round to the word "voiture d'eau" (water vehicle) which is used in the Charlevoix area to designate all the various types of boats, from the ice canoe, which ventures out on the winter ice, to the most immense of oil tankers that monopolize the dispossessed river. For the "goelettes", still precious indeed like a species in danger of becoming extinct, have been put in peril by human avarice. What name is to be given to a river that is deprived of these "goelettes" built of wood?

"... mes îles sont mortes et du mal
vert qu'ont les turquoises j'ai serti mes
bagues..."

Max Elskamp, Tour d'Ivoire

Having kept company with the artful works of the foam and with the sea urchins that offer returns difficult to cash in on, I said to Blanchon "In this home of yours, flowers are missing."

Not without pride, not without an air of mystery, he replied "Come and look at the sea's gardens."

We plunged into a large forest of sea algae that swayed back and forth with the ocean's secret breathing. Here the spoken word was not restricted to the rigours of form. Here nobody is limited to himself...

And the light so proud and straight, shattered now by surfaces, plunges beneath the water, skirts round objects, caresses the four breasts of a jellyfish and illuminates the countless imaginings of plankton.

I thought myself encircled by a forest fire on the edge of some lake where all the beasts of terror had taken refuge... or else locked in the secrets of a stained-glass world. Turning towards Blanchon, I found he had disappeared and, in his place, huge flakes of snow fell and fell into the bottomless depths.

Yet the snowflakes seemed also to turn, ascending towards the surface as if suspended on the balanced threads by a master puppeteer. I heard Blanchon's laughter echoed by all the strangely intermingling snowflakes, I heard Blanchon's voice saying "Light multiplies the sea." And it also makes the sounds multifold.

Suddenly, I found myself in the midst of a circle of images as if a single whale were reproduced to infinity by the luminous caress of the light. I called out to Blanchon "Where are you?" in order to destroy the bewitched mirage.

A petal detached from the immense flower that had faded away led me towards other gardens. And I understood that dream is not always illusion.

The Mournful Cry of the Lighthouse

One morning the fog! The boats which howl! The fear thick as smoke! The labours of Hercules have not lifted this fog!

Nothing shines, nothing gleams! In the circular hall of the horizons I am counfounded by the worst of unperceived difficulties the sea can hold — finding the right direction!

I thought the sea mocked me, so often did I hear it voice my thoughts. Fog! Fog! Fog! All the lighthouses shout their warning of fog as if trying to wake the phantoms of the deep.

Like a slender hope, a finback whale advances, horizonless, into the tightly cramped day.

On the white waters a blue bull bellows, plaintive and prophetic.

Nothing to gather here and even the imminent wrecks find refuge in unlikelihood.

For an entire day and an entire night we moved forward together, without a word said, expecting only prolonged silence from each other. We did not even exchange directions! We did not even believe in destinations, documents uncertain...

Off-shore from nothing and nobody!

On the blue waters a white bull grazes on the seaweed left by the wind and trumpets a warning of his presence. To give the sea a semblance of coherence.

> "Il est tard pour croire aux sirènes."
>
> Supervielle

In the heavens, Earth is but a far-off yet cherished fable that floats in the thin unstable air. And the stars know that Earth cannot for much longer hold out against the astronomy into which everything is plunged.

Free from care, Blanchon swims in the vertiginous pastures, breaking surface to breathe and share both conflicting elements, water and air.

On the liquid surface that nightly mirrors the stars, several islands scattered from the land, several fishing-boats moored to their nets, and the dangling webbed feet of a hundred "moyacks", eider ducks, swimming in search of black mussels.

Now and then we cross a riverbed which slumbers in the sandy depths. And then Blanchon ascends the currents to swim near the sand bars at the river's mouth. The row-boats and a few derelict schooners hear his call. As if he wanted to release the rivers and villages from captivity.

On the beach where children play, a purple butterfly engages in lively banter as it dances round the fingers of a young girl who has blonde hair.

In their mossy beds, pitcher plants gulp down millions of flies, and there are always more to pursue this fatal game of head-over-heels.

We inspect the villages of the gulf one by one and their similar troubles. Blanchon remarks, "They all have mornings, sandbars, docks on pilings, fishing-boats, children and worries."

Almost always we are pressed to stay longer... Yet we can do no more for them, only wish them what they call in their fondest memories and dreams "un beau naufrage" ("a wonderful wreck") to resolve the problems and precariousness of their existence.

Who can ever anticipate the course of those who navigate by their own reckoning.

A White Whale is a Mammal

One day a loud cry of distress! So Blanchon said, "Did you hear? That cry comes from an isle without defence."

I had not heard. Blanchon, forgetting the sea gardens, the countryside, events, and gentle words, swam hurriedly on.

From far-off we saw a scene of commotion. A woman alone with a wounded man. Two children playing at fishing and hunting in a cavity in the crag which served them as an islet and berth off-shore from all continents.

The man, while shooting at ducks with a gun too old and powder too black, had fractured his right arm and was talking away chaotically.

She who has never before taken the helm, sets out now to sea. The ducks and seagulls have already returned to their cove where they are fishing for shell-fish and sea urchins. The sun hovers near the horizon as if walking on the water.

I ask Blanchon anxiously, "Do you think she will make it home?" Blanchon, mysterious, replies "They will believe in a miracle."

Not without reason! The complicated wind blew the seamarks out of place and all night long the woman held fast the helm and steered the boat through the maze of black islets in the surrounding sea. Next morning, down on the wharf of the village where the hospital is located, people were saying: "She got through as easy as a fish."

"I am not a fish," commented my friend Blanchon, the white whale.

How can one not believe in sirens?

"La baie du Vieux Château"

In the heart of a bay sheltered by Cap Noir, looking almost like a plump oyster in its fat round shell, a docile little village sleeps in the folds of a faint mist.

Several sandpipers skit about nervously and shake their tail feathers as if looking for some excuse to fly. Blanchon says to me, "Look, it's over here."

I can see only the reflection of the present. In the fall the fishermen will return from the off-shore islands taking possession once again of their homes and the winter.

Blanchon has plunged several fathoms deep, just off Cap Noir, where a large ship buzzed with activity, it's crew climbing the rigging, casting the halyards, winding the winches, sliding along the length of the shrouds, jostling back and forth on the decks. I asked Blanchon' "Where are they bound for?"

Blanchon replied, "They have come safe into port."

And I thought to myself, there's no anchorage more perfect than in this harbour of legend.

Pirate Wreckers

The sea still has many solitudes to share. Vast spaces where no love dwells.

That day we were sailing round Anticosti to make some acquaintance with its phantoms. There is no kingdom on earth more fit for legends, fear, and pirate wreckers than this island with its almost inaccessible coastline. It is for this reason that it is named Anticosti.

An island that offers no ports and is the last refuge of an incomparable silence. Everything there brings paradise to mind; the wildlife ever present; the cliffs over-crowded with birds; almost an atmosphere of forbidden fruit; a majestic stag displaying his crown of antlers with head held high; and a vast solitude separating the keepers of the different lighthouses.

Have we depreciated the shipwrecks too much? Halfway up the reefs, I spied the look in the eyes of drowned men, I heard their last sighs, the rare quality of their dying words.

Blanchon asks, "With this gasp of breath and such eyes, do we yet know their faces?"

We are surrounded by many a wrecked ship. Wooden hulls like antiques furnishing deep dwellings in the reefs. Steel wrecks giving the impression of a vast, busy construction yard attacked by unceasing rust.

From a freighter loaded with porcelain goods that looks like some half-built hospital, several phantom workers suddenly rush out at the sound of noon bells ringing from the forecastle of an ancient schooner nearby still rocked by illusions.

Blanchon says to me, "Perhaps the breath of the sea-weed has given them new life."

Yet through a porthole there pokes the bristling mustache of stellar sea-cow, staring at us with the air of a foreman and inspecting my clean-shaved face with curiosity as if I'd been shipwrecked just yesterday.

From this meeting, I brought back a word that I will always keep like some precious object more valued than all the gold of discoveries. From now on, to speak of a fishing schooner sunken on the reefs it is the word "racqueuse" I will use, referring to a wreck jostled by the tide as it lays on the reefs. For why not let those who know what it is to be lost at sea have the right to name their shipwrecks themselves?

A Cape of Birds on Anticosti

For several days we sailed round this flower that had shipwrecks for petals. Sadness was a temptation.

A corsair ship lies at rest beside a "goelette". An old sailboat, still intact, carries on debate with the remains of a more recent ship! And sometimes, even a rowboat with all its oars and all its oarsmen but the helm broken!

That day the light was limpid, transparent to all differentiation. Water and air were so easy to confound that Blanchon, after lurching upwards had to redescend and consider the difference. We were drawing close to Pointe aux Bruyères, where there are lakes, peat-bogs, lobsters, roe-deer and a very high lighthouse built with French stone. I called out to Blanchon "Look, such a fine harbour yet so many boats are at berth in the roadstead!"

Soon I understood the difficulty reflected by this landscape of boats helter-skelter, at berth without anchorage in only twenty or thirty fathoms of water. The seals had taken up residence here. I asked Blanchon, "What has become of their gazing eyes?"

Blanchon, my friend the white whale, led me then to the nearest cape where thousands of gannets and seagulls were busy with their bird activities and passions.

Why should not those who know what it is to be shipwrecked have the right to name, in honour of these birds, this cape which is the land of their sea tragedy?

Sunrise

A little before daylight we heard a great stir and commotion of colours.

Blanchon, who was swimming sluggishly, mounted to the surface. There was neither tree nor drifting isle on the horizon.

Only a boat by itself and in the surrounding waters a confusion of ropes, winches and nets. A fisherman with an expression of amazement on his face was studying his catch in silence. Caught between the floating meshes of net, the dark coloured floats and the dangling oars, a large yellow fish splashed around in the water.

The boat was one of those "barges", as they were called, from Havre Saint-Pierre, with two masts and pointed at both ends. Only three or four boats like this can still be found and these already show the strains idleness forced on them and on all the North Shore.

So beautiful and so smooth were the hull and flanks of this skiff, the sun had taken it for a dead seagull.

Blanchon said to me, "The sun, when it rises from the water and the early morning, gathers up the dead seabirds to return them to the realm of light."

But why had this "barge" chosen the form of a dead seagull?

Blanchon replied, "Because it is like those fishermen grown old who do not want to drop off to sleep when running aground."

I thought to myself that it takes a great deal of love to be able to depart one night in search of such a morning.

And the sun rose on the sea and on a seagull in the form of a "barge" from Havre Saint-Pierre.

A Village of Many Isles

It was a June day and the gulf was full of enormous drift-ice broken free from the Strait of Belle-Isle that, in times gone by, was named Chasteaulx because of all these drifting white fortresses.

Each year the walruses' great palace cracks and breaks apart. And pieces of ice larger than islets float down to these riverbanks where they melt, their life trickling into the sea like a fountain singing of a magic world.

Near this drift ice flowing off-shore towards the open waters, an entire village was also setting out from its winter palace. And it was truly a departure of sea gypsies. Strings of boats towed seawards, each family's hustle and bustle, the boat for the chairs, and the one for the dogs, another for the children and the pots and pans and the seaweed pallets and all their paraphernalia.

Blanchon said to me "Tonight a whole village of the shores will become a village of the isles. A village of how many isles? A village all of isles—"toutes isles!""

And I realized that for these people the land was only prized through inadvertence. They were a people of the sea and they lived all summer long on the isles to be next to all seas.

Jacques Cartier
A King's Captain

il y a pareillement force grues, signes, oultardes, ouayes, cannes, allouettes, faisans, perdrix, merles, mauvez, turtres, chardonnereulx, serins, lunottes, rossignolz, passes solitaires et autres oiseaulx comme en France et en grant abondance.

Jacques Cartier

Three Sailing Vessels

To sail to the very edge of hazard and change the face of the world so much!

The men who achieved this, their saga is that of a dangerous seafaring life... Their navigation relied on mere hypotheses... And their sailing vessels were prey to every current of wind and water.

Yes, they had compasses and reckoning. Yes, some astronomy and cartography. Yes, they had measuring instruments of the most diverse kind from the "révélateur des profondeurs" and the "bâton de Lévi"—plumb lines and poles—to nocturlabes, chronometers, sundials and waterclocks. Yes, there were theories of the greatest variety and the greatest fantasy. Yes, indeed, and much else guided the navigating of discoveries!

Even so, and in spite of the pretensions of pilots and quartermasters, Samuel de Champlain indicates in his voyage report:

Dieu n'a pas permis à l'homme l'usage de la longitude. (God has not permitted man the knack of longitude.)

Certainly luck also stood in good stead of those who came safe into port after searching the stars for an indication of a return route from nowhere!

A Captain Judged by his Peers

How did Cartier and the others find their various routes among so many islets and so many seabirds?

Perhaps these men knew what the fishes and the whales know of the sea!

As well as facing the oceans without the knack of longitude, they still had to traverse bewildering and glorious legends of the mysterious sea and of wondrous islands.

Reality, often more dangerous than legend, awaited them west of the known world!

Another Captain who has navigated by sail — without compass, without maps, and without any star other than his own genius at reckoning — a Captain who has frequented the waters surrounding the islets and drift ice of the gulf, gave me his opinion of the first Captain of the river:

"Well, Jacques Cartier was a good navigator for certain, by what he did.

Cross the ocean, there's nothing difficult in that. To start with, there were others who had crossed it long before Jacques Cartier. They came right to the coast of Labrador to fish here. But what I can't help asking myself is how they could sail upstream from Blanc Sablon to Quebec without a map. They certainly didn't know about the reefs. They certainly didn't know about the channels. They didn't know about the shoals. They didn't know anything!

My idea of it is that he took a lot of time going upstream. And he sent his longboats out ahead to take soundings. While he was putting up his forts on shore.

In any case, he wasn't a superhuman he was just a man. Going up to Blanc Sablon, that's a giveaway that is. After that there are reefs though. Even in mid-sea you think you'll be able to go ahead and then suddenly there are reefs and you can't get by. Me, I'd say he sent his longboats to take soundings a couple of days then he sailed upstream to another harbour. Then they took soundings for another stretch ahead, then he went that stretch, and so on. It's like that or else he would have lost his ships, and he didn't lose them." (J.A.Z. Desgagné, Captain of the *Mont-Ste-Marie*, St-Joseph-de-la-Rive.)

A Captain who is accustomed to the time of sails and storms and to the islets unknown to mapmakers and hasn't lost a "goélette" in fifty years of sailing between Quebec and Blanc Sablon tells us this of another Captain from more ancient times whose name was Cartier!

And it is fair consideration! Navigators recognize the merits of the man who surveyed one of the most difficult country's of the sea, that of "toutes isles", that of the Mingan archipelago, that of the Caribou islets and Île aux Ouefs, that of the currents and reefs of the Saguenay, that of the group of isles I call "Archipel des Sorciers", located just east of Quebec City and west of Cap Tourmente where every spring the wild white geese come to nest and make love!

A Captain from St-Joseph-de-la-Rive who esteems Cartier's skill is this Captain of today, the last man to sail up and down this country of seabirds which is scarcely at its beginning!

To lose your ship, do you have to shipwreck yourself?

And without a ship what remains to be said of a river which, surely, makes us legitimate in our own eyes?

"... des ouiseaulx desqueulx y a si grant numbre que c'est une chose incréable qui ne le voyt..."

Jacques Cartier

It is on the shores of the St-Laurent (St. Lawrence), a vast reserve of landscapes and discoveries, that we're about to anchor our boats and our knowledge.

To begin with, there's the horizontal relief, deeply wrinkled, furrowed with troughs, cradled by sands, bordered by stones at water-level, by dwarf trees and giant bogs.

But to trick the vigilance of seafarers, there's also the great and exorbitant genus-tree of birds and, above all, the dense crowd of seabirds that claim their perch on the rocks like an assembly of parliamentarians looking for a common accord.

And, next, let's look at Cartier's report about these birds as he relates his contact with them and the newly found land:

"On the twenty first of May we set sail... until we came to the isle of birds (Isle des Ouaiseaulx)... this isle was surrounded by banks of ice broken up and drifting in pieces... In spite of the ice, our two longboats went to this island to have some of the birds, of which there are so many that it seems incredible unless you have been there to see. Though this isle is about one league in area, it is so full of birds that the ground seems planted with them... and there are a hundred times more flying in the air than on the ground."

Here then are birds so numerous as to be difficult to count. A resource of unmeasurable value!

On a land indifferent to all else, these birds must have been a welcoming sight. How could anyone resist such promise, how could one refuse this abundance of birdlife in all its varieties of form and flight and cries. How could one not have gone onto this land that resembled no other place, this land of birds for the taking?

And Cartier saw here what none of us ever will... a type of bird which could not fly and seemed almost to come to greet you with gestures and an air of hospitality. One can easily believe in their almost human kindness as Cartier vividly relates his astonishment:

"These birds are as large as geese, and black and white with a beak like a crow. And they are constantly in the sea and cannot fly in the air because they have small wings, half the size of a hand, yet in the water they go as swiftly as other birds do in the air. And there are birds so fat here that it is a marvel."

Marvellous birds, almost too human, these Great Auks, fat and noisy, "without wings" and "without teeth", abundant on these waters filled with islets and ice. But these flightless Great Auks of the time of the discovery had not foreseen the arrival of the three ships from St-Malo:

"We descended to the lower part of the smallest isle and in our longboats took away all of these birds that we could want. It would have been possible to fill thirty boats full in an hour. There are so many birds on this isle that all the ships of France could easily load up with provisions here without it being perceivable that any of the birds were killed."

This advice was soon followed and all the ships from France, or Navarre, or elsewhere, that were passing by stopped on Île des Oiseaux to restock their meat supplies before continuing with their fishing or their explorations.

Because birds are not enough to people the earth!

A Testament to Longitude and Latitude

Did he dream of making a country of these millions of birds, this man Cartier, who left us a testament to longitude and latitude and gannets and seagulls in which he used the finest of expressions to describe what could not be quantified:

Icelles isles étoient aussi très plaines d'oiseaulx que ung pré de herbe (These isles were filled with birds as a meadow is with grass)

Among these isles and so many birds, he had a choice to make. Either sail round the world to India, and in that case to set full sail out to the high seas... Or sail the nearby shores and see what report was to be made of this difficult land, and in that case he would have to stay to explore, observe to understand, predict the unknown to appreciate this place that was all of isles—"Toutes Isles".

But the sea holds us all through our unavowed desire for new and open spaces, through its inducement with offers—always to be realized tomorrow—which transcend us all. How could one resist sailing further on—"plus oultre"—into this sea passage?

For there's something that always pulls us to the sea, we were imagined and conceived there millenniums ago and its salt is in our blood just as a fish also carries its own oceans within itself... And we are always ready to exchange even the risk of death with the sea. As if the distance of our voyage could make us equal to something.

How can one tame the distances and stay to possess them, to fence them in like a garden of the highest importance?

How can one not bite down, with gleaming teeth, with loud voice, into the flesh of the fruited wind?

How can ont tame the distances and stay to possess them, to fence them in like a garden of the highest importance?

But sometimes it is necessary to resign oneself to exploring a land of birds so as to not irremediably forget to gather history itself like so many eggs.

The mysteries and superabundance of islets, coves, rivers, birds and mountains having been weighed in his heart, Cartier spoke the most beautiful of words that one can say to any land, be it still new or already ancient:

Et pour ce que voullion abvoir plus emple cognoissance desdits paroiges, mismes les voiles bas et en travers. (And because we wanted to have more ample knowledge of this area, we lowered sail to broach the shore.)

To respond to the "plus oultre"—to that which is further on—isn't it necessary to decide first on the unquantifiable.

Cosmography

The world where Cartier was a King's Captain had just come to realize its own profile, in a sense, with the increasing proof that the world is round and always has been.

Cartier, in the second narration about his voyage, gives us his testimony of this overwhelming fact that seems to expand the world through really it is shrinking it, closing it in upon itself and its own rotundity like a snail in the orbit of its spiral shell:

J'allégué ce que davant, pour ce que je regarde que le souleil, qui, chaincun jour se lêve à l'orient et se recouse à l'occident, faict le tour et circuyt de la terre, donnant lumière et chaleur à tout le monde en vingt quatre heures, qui est ung jour naturel.

Cartier, with all of these careful explanations in regard to the sun, affirms that the earth is round. And in every sense. Yet knowing all of this we still will never be able to appreciate vividly enough these ancient words of a navigator.

So Cosmographers of the time were engaged in the task of writing the first fabulous poems about this new Earth though they actually did not know how the sea managed to turn round it. And the boats turn round it too, without falling off.

Geography in one single stroke learned of all its limits before even examining them in detail and now sought its future in the stars and in embellishments of its maps and drawings.

It is not surprising that certainty, in such conditions, is influenced by fable and takes on the cloak of legend. It was then that whales swallowed sailing vessels of sixty tonne and more. It was then that narwhales impaled ships. And then that departures were not preoccupied with the homecoming, because the voyage was worth as much as life if the portulans, the maps of the two hemispheres and the printed drawings were to be believed.

Without hope of marvels ahead, who would have dared to sail through the sea of storms? Without the mystery, who would have penetrated the secret? Nonetheless, the unanswerable astrolabe left nothing to chance. But chance was sufficient unto itself.

The People ... The Ice

However, the land was not living up to its promises of birds and abundance, and the blunt words he pronounced first claiming the shores of the gulf had not lost any of their bluntness:

Si la terre estait aussi bonne qu'il y a bons hables se serait ung bien; mais elle ne se doibt nommer Terre Neuffve, mais pierres et rochiers effrables et mal rabottéz; car en toute ladite coste du nort, je n'y vy un charetée de terre, et si descendy en plusieurs lieux...

Fors à Blanc Sablon, il n'y a que de la mousse, et de petits bouays avorté...

Fin, j'estime mieulx que aultrement que c'est la terre de Dieu donna à Cayn. Il y a des gens à la dit terre...

He adds, not without astonishment, this phrase ("Il y a des gens à la dit terre"—There are people on this said land) as incredible on this sunny June day of our times as on that sunny June day when Cartier came by, nearly five centuries ago.

Because, indeed, there are people on the said land, stony and rugged as it is. People by the harsh sea where nothing belongs to anyone, from the Mingan archipelago right up to Blanc Sablon. People who give their lives to fishing in summer, to forests in winter, and to luck when it happens.

The "Calculot"

We had already sailed with chance discoveries but all the sea had resembled nothing more than sea deprived of legend and conveniently made for ships that know the end of the journey.

It is then that we came upon Île aux Perroquets, close to Blanc Sablon, where Cartier reports:

Il y a grant nombre de richards qui ont le bec et les pieds rouges et hairent dedans des pertuis soubs terre, comme connins.

Near a village of cod fishermen, on a sandbank isle, this village of seabird spearfishers.

The sun and a raised horizon from this flat isle, the shape of an anvil, where as Cartier says there are always large numbers of birds which, like hares, dig themselves burrows under the rocks or in the peat, out of reach of hunters of fresh eggs.

Plump and with short wings, these Atlantic Puffins, are avid fishers of sand-eels. They are also called sea-parakeets and, even better: "calculots".

An old Breton word this word "calculot" that took root long ago in the sea foam of our isles and it brings to mind for us the fate that the sailors of St-Malo, La Rochelle and elsewhere brought to the Atlantic Puffin's cousin, the Great Auk, of which Cartier talks about in terms of their good-will:

Sont iceulx oiseulx si gras que c'est une chose merveilleuse et icelle isle, étant aussi très plaine de ces ouaiseaulx que ung pré de herbe... tous les navires de France y pourroyent facillement charger sans que on s'apperceust que l'on en eust tiré... en chargèrent deux barques en moins de demye heure dont chaincun de noz navires en sallèrent quatre ou cinq pippes, sans compter ce que nous en peusmes mangier de froys.

Nothing is more ephemeral... and nothing has more tenacity... than these ship's names... than these children learning about fishing... in a disobliging country which knows not where the sea begins... nor where the land ends... and how the sea will surge or subside... only that it is everywhere... and the land in the midst of the tides... and the tides bring the white foam of reefs and shipwrecks...

Because there are people on the land, and reason to be astonished when one considers that at Blanc Sablon it is necessary to uproot the dwarf trees to get firewood from the gnarled and twisted roots that the people there call "caribou horns" in their own language.

There are people on the land, and they devote their lives completely to the opens seas, to facing the blue where seagulls, gannets and pilot whales are to be found... and the iceberg palaces of the walruses, sculpted by a million suns... and there is a story told that sometimes tormented by grief these palaces capsize making a sound like a bird's cry which throws the waves into confusion...

Wherefore ship's have blamed the white whales for shipwrecks.

In the end it was plain to see. And a hundred years ago it was definite that not a single Great Auk was left on these isles, the Great Auk, once as abundant as grass in a meadow, is now extinct.

I could not help but feel a child's regret for this beautiful broken toy, the Great Auk of my country of times past.

To console us, however, each spring brings back the "calculot" related to the "Great Auk". As many as fifty thousand of them arrive at the same isle in this epoch when villages of birds are dying out.

When I thought of this word "calculot", I had the impression of a past wealth returning. Enriched by possession of this word that will hold fast to my very speech, I knew I was well-rewarded for my voyage. For we owe nothing to chance.

But the name of a bird is not enough to convey the history of a whole river.

A Meeting

Did Cartier suspect at all the wealth gathered by the currents and migrations in this sea that in other respects has few human qualities, or did he perhaps simply wish to keep the secret.

It is sufficient to listen to the following report contained in *Les Relations* to be convinced that Cartier was not inventing the voyage:

estans à icelle baie de Napetipi nous aperseumes ung grant navire, qui estoit de la Rochelle, qui avoit passé la nuyt le hable de Brest, où il pensoit aller faire sa pescherie; et ne s'avoient où ilz estoient. Nous allames à bort, avecques noz barques, et le mysmes dedans ung aultre hable, à une lieue plus à ouest.

Thus, Cartier, a King's Captain tells of meeting a large ship hailing from La Rochelle and seeking a route to the sea.

Cartier indicated the route and found that this Captain knew of the Havre du Brest as a fishing ground.

What will become of this encounter? Cartier, a King's Captain and from St-Malo, talking about this new land and exchanging information with the men of this cod-fishing boat.

What will become of this Havre de Brest which was to be found in the Baie du Vieux Château and where, legend reports, the fishing season gathered some ten thousand people and more than a hundred ships?

What will become of the fishing for cod, the hunting of seals, the slaughtering of the Great Auk, and this meeting on the 12th of June in the year 1534.

So true it is that a discoverer is not necessarily the first to come to a new land.

An Epoch

I could not help but feel the melancholy of these chance events for which there is no longer any good fortune, as if the sailing vessels of yore had exhausted all the contingencies of space before our advent.

We were sailing along the coast of the bay of Brador, which is as bare as a cathedral before the approach of the thousands of sculpting hammers.

Sometimes the presence of a steeple to serve as a landmark like the Cross of ancient explorers.

Sometimes, too, a few houses linked to the sea by a few boats.

And then hardly anything which starts anew on the scale of the country. How do we believe that we are navigating the imminence?

And is it true that the hues of dusk were plotting events around the white sailing boats of Blanc Sablon, designing their return from the fishing grounds.

Around house so white and so close to the sea as possible that they seemed almost on the point of sailing out to greet the white boats returning.

Dissatisfied with the hurried advance of the night, I evoked a memorable meeting, the three schooners of St-Malo or else a schooner for cod fishing that hailed from La Rochelle. And I pondered the fact that though the seabirds remained—except for the Great Auks—the sailing vessels of times gone by had abandond their voyages, leaving us with hands empty and without memory.

It was then, sailing into this harbour at Blanc Sablon, that I spied three schooners which hailed from Lunenburg, Nova Scotia. They were at anchor in this far-off harbour for the night and would make these waters their fishing grounds in the morning.

We had both no doubt mistaken the epoch... Was it necessary to turn back? To correct the itinerary? And where would I sail to on the open sea?

Trying to deciper the yellow letters on the prow of the black ships.

On the point of forcing fate and abusing chance, I held on by a miracle to my illusions. An instant later I believed myself to be "ce grand navire qui estoit de La Rochelle" meeting, on the ancient sea, the King's ships with ermine names.

In truth, I was seeing three fishing boats beside the quay, three two-masted schooners, black hulls...

And the names up near the hawse-hole in scroll and arabesques: the Sherman Zwicker, the Arthur J. Lynn, the John L. Zwicker. All three out of Lunenberg, Nova Scotia... All three from fishing and from fog were as much sailing ships of legend as any ship could be.

They were three schooners. And three Captains with beards that were black and voices that were haughty.

What will become of these rugged crews, leading a life of pirates and fatigue, and who have lost forever the desire to shave, to dress well, to be moved by pity. And these seafarers toss every early morning into the sea as they haul in the lines and cast them out again into the day that has hardly begun. Two by two, on fragile dorys, to haul in the lines and empty the sea, cod by cod.

They were three schooners... And one fine night in the setting sun performing the flamboyant act of filleting...

The three schooners, the three ships (always the same three ships) quivering with the gleaming gestures...

And the filleters disembowelling the slimey cod, scatter them on the decks, knee-deep. Others hose down the cod to wash off the slime. Others load them into the hode. All surrounded by the sun's rays like ropes through the rigging.

And the entrails, white orgy, cast into the sea and adrift!

Time hurries them! The men, in yellow oilskins red with blood and sunlight, covered with slime and shouting and knives, precipitate gestures and swear words to make a bed, a large white bed, for their giddy weariness.

Is their, on all Earth, weariness comparable to this day of work which lasts as long as the sun stays in the sky of a June day.

On the sea, redder than the fishing, a few dories haul in their black nets to take capelin as bate.

Huge containers full of silver ingots give the quay with its shouts and cries the busy air of a fish-market filled with gleaming white fish.

The lights go on over the gray decks where the sun becomes lost in the blood and water left by the tragedy.

And the chorus of ancient gestures and seafaring voices weary from recent strains continues late into the night like a sacrificial rite, immemorable and of daily occurrence. Still another hour or two of this quivering about after the setting of this June sun, before the dreamless and secretless night of the fishermen stunned by the breadth and the length of time: as if the sun was not their most mortal enemy.

In this way then, like a King's Captain whose ship is laden down with discoveries and seabirds, we met that day three schooners out of Lunenberg on a sea too easy to believe deserted... Three schooners continuing the legend on land and sea abounding in marvels...

And will the present once again resemble memories.

Sea of Sand

Sea sown with isles,
land sown with waters!
why do you so often look
where nothing is happening?

A flight of "moyacks" white, as if the foam had wings,
spreads far and wide: they detour around ships, scattered by love, fruit forever ripe of land without fruit-
trees.

Sea sown with isles
land sown with waters!
why do you so often look
where nothing is happening?

Three ships, off-shore from a morning surrounded by
fog, fish the silence too vast for one man alone: three
black ships fish the waters then stray distant from my
thoughts, precious fruit of hazard, the most improba-
ble and the most certain of all fruit.

Sea sown with isles
land sown with waters
and all the efforts of stone
to defy time.

Why have you imagined so marvellously an unserviceable country? Because one has to sell one's fish.

For ships only sail to the ends of the earth in hope of
finding the orchard that bears golden fruit. And
nobody prefers cod.

The earth was continuing its stone-hearted legend:
vast mountain graveyard, perfect silence that one
can't rely on, immutable sands that slit the throat of
sleeping coves behind sandbars.

But man lives by words! And once more I saw the villages clinging to their village names and the isles
clinging to their names of isles reminding me of
Cartier's words:

et le jour Saint-Barnabé, après la messe onye, nous
allasmes avec nos barques oultre le dit hable de Brest à
ouest découvrir et voir quels hables il y avoit. Nous
passames parmy les îles qui sont en si grant nombre,
qu'il n'est possible les sçavoir nombréz... pourquoi...
lesdites isles furent nommées Toutes Isles.

From Blanc Sablon to Sept Iles, names on the map
express but uncertain guidemarks, fraught with
apprehensions...

and between the words and between the villages, this
vast emptiness to put into words, to translate, an
emptiness filled with seabirds, dangers, and driftwood
shaped like the bow of a ship...

on beachers where sometimes someone will stop off in search of an isle to complete the discovery of the New World!

Doesn't it seem like the land was just left there in its original state of creation: a vast green silence... the harbour where a river idles... and the air filled with the strong stink of seaweed rotting in the opulence...

land scarcely escaped from the sea, and still moved to pity by the eyes of the waves, disputed, userviceable, grandiose land where villages of seabirds hide and the spell of shipwrecks of unknown cause...

sea scarcely escaped from the land where sometimes, toutes îsles all of isles, effort of our archipelagos, hides man's villages...

toutes îles all of isles, let me tell
your sweet-sounding names!

île de La Demoiselle in a bay of des Belles-Amours!
île du Vieux Château
île de la Tête à la Baleine
île du grand Mécatina
and waters sewn with des îles Harrington
île aux Perroquets
îles Affligées
îles du Défunt Français

toutes îsles all of isles, let me decorate your unnamed isles with names...

île de la lune, for the moon
île du soleil, for the sun
île du dernier naufrage, for the last shipwreck
île de la prochaine tempête, for the next storm
îles des grandes échoueries, for ships run aground

environment of isles to recite, to sing, to explore, the stuff of legends, toutes isles all of isles.

What is to be done with so many words spoken unclaimed? For my sole pleasure have I not imagined myself seigneur de cette seigneurie, lord of these lands, for my pleasure and also to preserve words for they give villages a face, but others will come, with their Church and their chimneys, making me a stranger in my country for lack of words to tell.

But one day the village will take revenge upon the principalities!

And the villages will take back their humanity!

And the county of Duplessis will by full right become the country of *Toutes isles* to give the poetry and the language of the people from here precedence over the sad history of the princes from elsewhere!

One day... soon... when finally the future takes root on the naked surface of miseries and, like lichen, transforms into humus the sterile stones of capitulation on a land that God gave to Cain.

Pierre Perrault, cinematographer and poet, was born in Montreal in 1927. His most widely known works include the films: *Pour la suite de monde*; *Le Règne du jour*; *L'Acadie, l'Acadie*. Several collections of his narratives and poetry have been published, including the book *Toutes Isles* from which the preceding works were taken. His poetry also includes collections entitled: *Portulan*; *Ballades du temps précieux*; *En désespoir de cause*; *Chouennes*; et *Gelivures*.

1

3

6

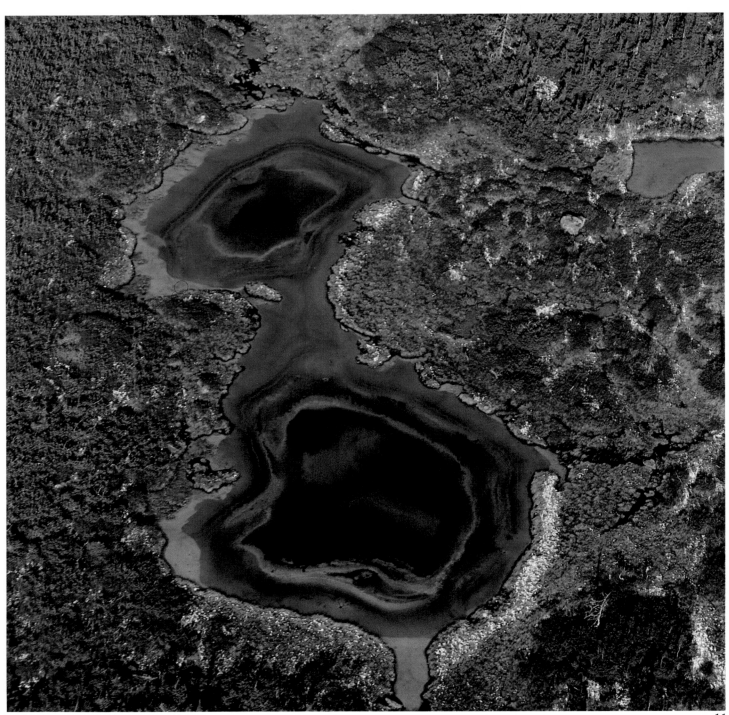

18

21

23

26

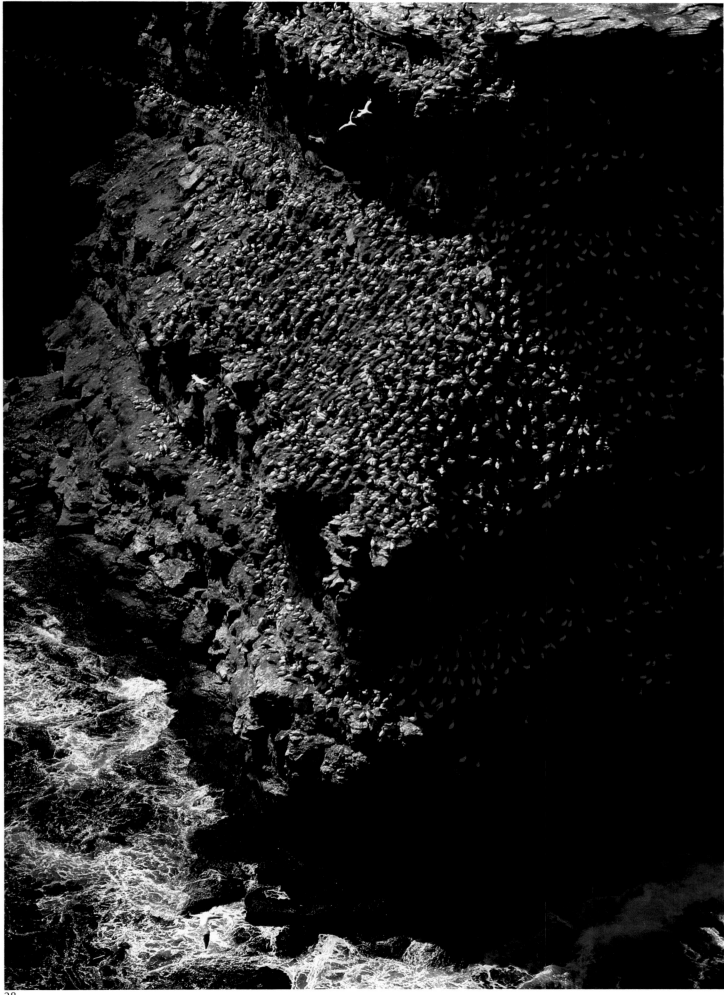

33

36

39

48

50

56

58

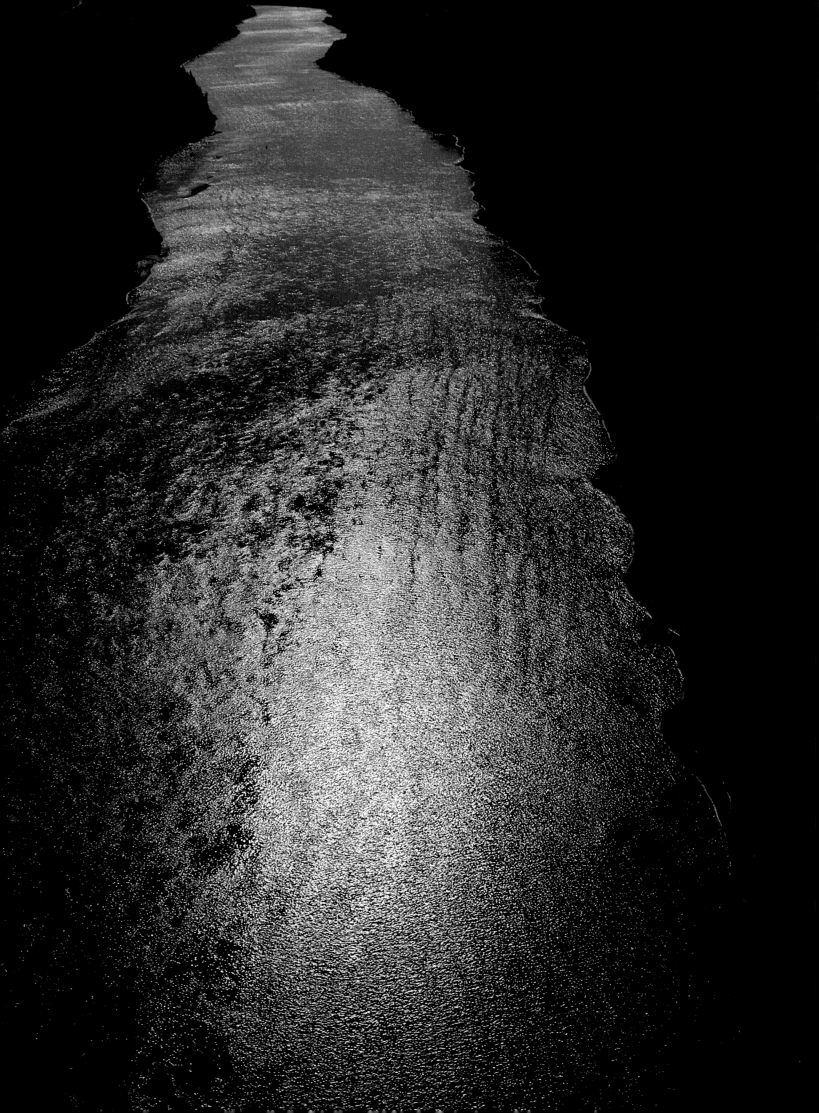

63

69

73

80

83

91

101

103

107

116

123

133

134

138

The Saint-Laurent

Linking the Atlantic to the interior of the North American continent, the Saint-Laurent (St. Lawrence) is a superb natural river route which has its source in Lake Superior and runs 2 632 kilometres to the sea. This sea passage leading directly to the Great Lakes follows a practically straight path, an advantage that makes the river route even more exceptional in comparison with other major rivers of the same size throughout the world.

The northern shore of the Saint-Laurent includes the spectacular landscape of the Canadian Shield, and the southern shore touches on the Appalachian Mountains. Here, then, is an impressively beautiful waterway.

An integral part of the Laurentian hydrographic network, the Saint-Laurent has another characteristic feature. At its source, the river is scarcely differentiated from the surrounding lake system and, likewise, the great estuary at river's end is scarcely differentiated from the Gulf and the sea.

The Saint-Laurent is also the major waterway for maritime navigation from the North Atlantic. It opens on the Gulf, which is located at the same latitude as the English Channel, the 50th parallel; on the Atlantic it is at the closest point to the European coastline. Compared to the Hudson's Bay and Mississippi river networks, it provides the shortest route between Europe and the centre of North America. It has, therefore, played a major role in international relations and intercontinental trade. Because of the link it provides with the Great Lakes as well as its own major tributaries such as the Saguenay, the Richelieu, and the Outaouais, and because of its proximity and accessibility to other major hydrographic networks, the Saint-Laurent is an ideal strategic point of access to the interior territory of the entire North American continent.

From the Great Lakes to the Gulf

In the geographic area from Lake Ontario to the Hochelaga archipelago, the Saint-Laurent starts its course in the basin of the Great Lakes where, in the Thousand Islands region, it still very much resembles a lake itself. After this point the water is swift-running and the riverbed is faulted and buckled. It is this part of the river that includes the international rapids and, after a stretch of calm water at Lac Saint-François, the Saint-Laurent meets its major tributary, the 1 115 kilometres Outaouais. Choppier waters then lead to the Lachine Rapids.

Between Montreal and Quebec City, the river is transformed and becomes a calm but powerful force. The riverbed levels after the Lachine Rapids but the water is only at 7 kilometres above sea level in the port of Montreal. Further back at Johnston Bridge it had been at an altitude of 74 metres. Near Montreal, the litre per hour flow is at the rate of 8 500m³/s. From here to Quebec City, the surrounding terrain mostly consists of plains and low plateaus. At Sorel, the Saint-Laurent joins its longest southern tributary, the Richelieu, which drains the waters of Lake Champlain. Further east at Pointe du Lac, another large tributary, the Saint-Maurice, runs down from the Canadian Shield on the north. Gradually, the Saint-Laurent is widening. At Trois Rivières its shores lie only about 2 kilometres apart. By the time it reaches Donnacona, the river spans 4 kilometres from shore to shore but is still not at its full width. Steep cliffs bank both shores of the river at Quebec City, narrowing it to only 1 kilometre across. Nevertheless, the waters are as deep as 50 kilometres here and the flow is at an impressive rate of 10 000m³/s.

Downstream from Île d'Orléans is where dramatic changes occur. It is here that the Saint-Laurent becomes an estuary. It is here that it widens to twenty kilometres. It is here that its water flows into brine currents and becomes a salty sea with tides of an amplitude of 4 to 6 metres. The shoreline changes too. The rolling lowlands disappear. The contours of the land rise abruptly here. This is the steep and beautiful landscape of Charlevoix. This is the tableland of the Laurentian Plateau, reaching a height of 1 175 metres above sea level. But this is still not enough. The Saint-Laurent now widens and deepens. At the Saguenay it deepens to more that 300 metres. By Baie-Comeau it widens to as much as 60 kilometres. And, at Pointe des Monts, it grows to full width with more than 100 kilometres of water stretching across from Sept Îles to the Gaspé coast. From there, like when it first left the Great Lakes, the Saint-Laurent flows to its final transformation with such discrete and natural ease that it is difficult to even discern as it joins the Gulf.

St. Lawrence Ports

In Canada and the United States, there are 32 ports along the St. Lawrence and the Great Lakes. Some ports are industrial or commercial centres, some specialize in lumber shipments and some are stopover points. Among the largest ports are those in Montréal, Sorel, Trois-Rivières, Québec, Baie-Comeau, Port-Cartier, Sept-Îles and Havre-Saint-Pierre.

Montréal Harbour, administered by Ports Canada, is halfway between the mouth of the St. Lawrence and the Lakehead. Grain, crude petroleum and heating oil are among the main imports and exports. Average depth at the many wharves is 10,7 metres. The statistics for 1981 give a good picture of port activity in Montréal. Total tonnage was 24,800,000 tonnes (grain 6.2 million, petroleum products 6.7 million, dry and liquid bulk cargo 6.7 million, container cargo 3.5 million, other general cargo 1.6 million). Montreal Harbour has three grain elevators with a combined capacity of 550,000 tonnes.

The port of Sorel, at the mouth of the Richelieu River, is a public port administered by Transport Canada.

Its western boundary is also the eastern boundary of the Port of Montréal. Sorel's main exports are grain, scrap metal, steel ingots and titanium oxide. The main imports are coal, grain, molasses, heating oil, pulp and titanium ore. Depths at the wharves range from 6,1 to 9,1 m. Total shipments in 1980 were 7.2 million tonnes.

The Port of Trois-Rivières, administered by Ports Canada, was built where the Saint-Maurice River flows into the St. Lawrence. The leading exports are newsprint, grain, asbestos and aluminum products. The main imports are coal, pulpwood, sulphur, clay, salt and coke.

The Port of Québec City is also administered by Ports Canada. The main exports are grain, asbestos, ore and concentrates, lumber, newsprint, wood pulp, cement and food products. Imports include coal, heating oil, gasoline, fertilizer and salt.

Located on the north shore of the St. Lawrence, Baie-Comeau has a public wharf administered by Transport Canada. A newsprint mill and an aluminum smelter are established nearby.

The Port-Cartier Harbour, on the western side of Pointe Sainte-Marguerite, belongs to Québec Cartier Mining Co., which uses the facilities to ship iron ore concentrates. A railway links the mine to the port.

Sept-Îles boasts a deep-water port where freighters take on large shipments of iron ore from mines in Labrador.

Finally, the Port of Havre-Saint-Pierre is used mostly by Quebec Iron and Titanium Co. to ship ore. The dock is 198 metres long and the minimum draft 7,9 metres. Installations include a mineral ore conveyor belt, a loading tower and a crane.

Chronology

- 5000   The St.Lawrence River is born on an ancient sea-bed.

- 5000 to - 1000   After the last glaciation had moved northward, and the Champlain Sea that covered the St.Lawrence Valley had receded, the first Indians appeared. They are considered to be the first "Quebec" Indians and are classified in the culture so-called "archaic".

- 100   The St.Lawrence River becomes the principal emissary of the Great Lakes.

1100 to 1400   The Vikings settle in Greenland and visit the Gulf region, the St.Lawrence Valley and the Great Lakes.

1500   European fishermen (from the Basque country, La Rochelle and Brittany) sail off the coast of Newfoundland and at the entrance of the Gulf.

1534   Jacques Cartier's first voyage to Canada where he explores the Gulf of St.Lawrence.

1535-1536   Jacques Cartier's second voyage. After discovering the St.Lawrence River, he sails up to the island of Montreal.

1541   During his third voyage, Jacques Cartier goes up the St.Lawrence, and then the Outaouais River as far as Long-Sault.

1541-1543   Founding of Charlesbourg-Royal, at Cap-Rouge.

close to 1550   Basque whalers found the settlement of Île aux Basques.

1550-1600   The Iroquois people leave the St.Lawrence Valley and are replaced by the Algonquins.

1597   Charles Leigh tries to establish an English colony in the Magdalen Islands, but his project fails, opposed by the French, Basque and Micmac occupants.

1600   Founding by Pierre Chauvin of the first permanent establishment, at Tadoussac.

1603   Samuel de Champlain explores the St.Lawrence River beyond the island of Montreal.

1608   Founding of Quebec city by Samuel de Champlain.

1609-1634   Samuel de Champlain explores the Richelieu River and the Outaouais.

1634   Founding of Trois-Rivières by Laviolette.

1635   The Jesuits offer the first courses in hydrography in their Quebec College.

1642   Founding of Montreal by Paul Chomedey de Maisonneuve.

1646-1647   First mention of "Royal pilot in this country" and "River pilot".

1651-1793   Exploration of the continent, starting at the St.Lawrence River.

1658-1686   Exploration of the Great Lakes.

1669-1670   Exploration of the upper St.Lawrence.

1700   Construction of a canal in the Saint-Pierre River.

1731   Nomination of the first official pilot to Île Verte (Green Island) and first probing of the St.Lawrence River.

1760-1761   James Cook prepares the first summary of the St.Lawrence River's and Estuary's sea floor.

1768   In a regulation, Governor Murray declares the Bic official piloting station.

1784   Arrival of the first Loyalists on the left bank of the upper St.Lawrence, and creation of the first townships.

1796   First American settlement on the right bank of the upper St.Lawrence, at Ogdensburg.

1806   Construction of the first lighthouse on the St.Lawrence at Île Verte.

1844   Work on the shipping channel in middle St. Lawrence starts.

1848   Completion of a network of canals between Montreal and Kingston.

1901   Completion of a network of canals between Montreal and lake Érié designed to receive ships 78 metres long.

1909   Creation of the International Joint Commission.

1932   Presentation of Sir Alexander Gibb's report, which was going to give birth to the National Harbours Board and to the construction of eight locks in the Welland Canal, offering a seaway 7,60 metres deep, capable of welcoming ships 218 metres long.

1940   First studies by the Canadian Government on the serveying of ice floes in the Gulf of St.Lawrence.

1954-1959   Construction of the St.Lawrence Seaway.

1 Grand Banks

Le Banc qui s'appelle ainsi est une grande montagne qui est dans la mer et sous l'eau distante de vingt-cinq lieuës ou environ de l'Isle de Terre neufve, d'où la moluë verte prend son nom. Ce Banc a environ cent cinquante lieuës d'un bout à l'autre, et quelques cinquante lieuës en son plus large. Cette montagne qui est en la mer a au dessus d'elle en son plus haut vingt-cinq brasses d'eau, et en d'autres endroits trente, trente cinq, quarante, cinquante, et soixante brasses d'eau. Tout autour elle est coupée quasi tout droit, et en ce tour-là on ne trouve point de fonds à douze et quinze cens brasses de cordages; par là vous pouvez juger de la hauteur de la montagne qui est de roche, tout le haut en est plat quoy qu'elle aille en baissant, c'est où se pesche la moluë qui y trouve pour sa nourriture force coquillages de plusieurs sortes et d'autres poissons. Celuy-cy et fort glouton, et sa gourmandise s'étend sur tout, mesme sur ceux de son espece, et souvent on en pesche qui ne laissent pas depuis qu'ils sont pris à l'hameçon, dans le temps que l'on les tire en haut d'avaler à demy un de leur semblable si il se rencontre à son chemin; il ne trouve rien de trop dur, quelques-fois les pescheurs, laissent tomber leurs coûteaux: leurs mitaines, ou autres choses, si une moluë le rencontre elle l'avalle, et bien souvent ils peschent la moluë qui aura avallé ce qui sera tombé et le retrouvent dans son estomac, que les matelots appellent gau. Ce poisson a encore une propriété, qui est que ce qu'il avale qui ne se peut pas digerer, il le fait revenir de son gau qu'il retourne hors sa gueule, et en fait sortir tout ce qui luy nuit, aprés quoy il le retire en dedans, et ravalle cet estomac. Ceux qui vont ordinairement pour faire cette pesche sont des Normands du havre de Honfleur, de Dieppe, et d'autres petits havres de Normandie, mesme de Boulogne et de Calais, de Bretagne, d'Olonne et de tout le païs d'Aulnis: tout cela fait bien le nombre de deux cens à deux cens cinquante navires pescheurs tous les ans, et toute leur pesche n'est quasi que pour Paris, du moins les trois quarts.

Nicolas Denys
La pesche des moluës

2 Seagull

These big seagulls have a wide wingspan, a fan tail and a thick hooked beak. They are found in colonies along the coast and in harbours, where they fly in circles and squeal constantly. They touch down on the water to feed off flotsam or to pounce on fish. They follow ships but never stray far from shore.

3 Bluenose II

Ships and sailors in the *Bluenose Fleet* had their heyday in the 19th Century. The ships, built in Yarmouth, N.S., were equipped either with fore-and-aft sails or square sails. The *Bluenose II* is a replica of the famous fishing schooner that won many international races in the twenties and thirties.

4 Île aux loups
This remote speck of land is connected to Grindstone Island (île du Cap-aux-Meules) and Grosse-Île by surf-swept sand dunes. Many ships with full sails broke up here in wind storms.
Damase Potvin
Le Saint-Laurent et ses îles

5 Bonavista Cape
A statue of John Cabot, one of the European explorers who came before Jacques Cartier, stands on Bonavista Cape, Newfoundland, where he is believed to have dropped anchor in 1497.

6 Cuckold Cove
The greatest dangers for the ships approaching the eastern coast of Canada are icebergs, drift ice and ice banks carried by the Labrador current. Frequent fog around the ice fields of Nova Scotia and Newfoundland increase the danger.
Instructions nautiques,
Golfe et fleuve Saint-Laurent.

7 Strait of Belle Isle
Cartier, "the King's captain and pilot", was instructed to travel to the New Lands, "past the strait of Bay des Chasteaulx". The strait in question is the Strait of Belle Isle, between the north shore of Newfoundland and Labrador, at first mistaken for a bay, later recognized as a strait when fishermen looking for codfish kept going north without reaching the end. Cartier, an accomplished navigator, knew perfectly well this strait existed and may even have explored it.
Jean Tanguay
Le monde de Jacques Cartier

8 Cape Spear
Cape Spear is the easternmost tip of North America. This part of Newfoundland was linked to what is now Europe 250 million years ago.

9 Île du Gros Mécatina
The existence of a current coming through the Strait of Belle Isle is confirmed by the presence of ice-packs carried in the St. Lawrence every year despite southwestern winds. At times, the current takes them all the way to Mécatina, that is 200 kilometres from the mouth of the strait and 120 kilometres from the narrowest part at Pointe Amour, and even to the eastern tip of Anticosti Island. It is probably a branch of the great current coming from Davis which runs along the coast of Labrador and, every year, carries numerous icebergs southward.
P. Fortin
Sailing direction for the
Gulf and River St. Lawrence

10 **Funk Island**
Funk Island is a sanctuary for more than one million "marmettes" even though it barely covers 27 hectares. Puffins, gades, gannetts and gulls are also found here.

11 **Norris Point**
The Dorset Inuit civilization, which flourished from the dawn of the Christian era to 700 A. D., stretched northward along the coast of Newfoundland from Norris Point.

12 **Pointe Granite**
Out of the 87 toponyms used by Cartier during his first two voyages, 27 are still in use in the same areas where they were originally given. These 27 names were translated into modern French but they are the same, except for three pertaining to Newfoundland: "Karpont" became Quirpon, "Raze" Race, and "Rougnouze" Renews. Out of these 87 toponyms, 46 were invented by Cartier.
Christian Morissonneau
Le monde de Jacques Cartier

13 **Long Range Mountains**
Thousands of years ago, in Newfoundland, the Long Range Mountains emerged on the horizon. Erosion and ice age upheavals gave them their present shapes, carving up the basins at Western Brook and Baker's Brook and turning St. Paul's Inlet into a fjord. After the glaciers drifted away, the coastal plain stretching between the mountains and the sea began rising. This trend continues.

14 **Gros Morne Park**
Gros Morne Park was named after the second-highest mountain on the Island of Newfoundland. This summit, rising 806 metres above the dark waters of Bonne Bay, is often covered with snow or shrouded in clouds or fog.

15 **Western Brook**
The mixed and unusual forms of flora found in Gros Morne Park reflect the proximity of the Gulf of St. Lawrence, the diversity of soils and the shallow bedrock. In the Long Range Mountains—once known as *mons des Granches* after the family name of Jacques Cartier's wife or, perhaps, because of their barn-like shape—the drying effect of the winds and the altitude produce vegetation similar to tundra, broken up by moss-covered rocks.

16 **Western Brook**
The Western Brook gorge is a good example of the effects of glaciers. Inside the fjord we find a lake fed by waterfalls, some more than 90 metres high.

17 Ten Mile Lake

To the north of the mountain top you can see traces of the last glacial period of Newfoundland. The plateau disappears into a deep gorge where a river once flowed along a wide crevice. The shifting glacier streams carved the ancient river bed that now forms a U-shaped valley. When the glaciers melted away, this fjord became linked to the sea. This link with the sea eventually was blocked by a soil buildup and, today the lake consists of fresh water.

18 Tableland

Located to the south of Bonne Bay, Tableland, also known as *Le plateau*, supports very little vegetation. Like other peaks in the Long Range Mountains, it is inhabited by Labrador caribou, white-headed eagles, sea eagles and gyrfalcons.

19 Baie de Blanc-Sablon

The bay of Blanc-Sablon, situated at the entrance of the Strait of Belle Isle, derives its name from the white sand of a river that flows into the bay. The Au Bois and Greenly Islands partly shelter it from the southwestern winds that make the sea very stormy in that area.

20 Longue Pointe

Between Longue Pointe—near the village of Lourdes-de-Blanc-Sablon—and Cape Whittle, the coastline is shaped by the sound and the bays dotted with islands, and rocky reefs abruptly rising from deep waters to a few metres above the surface. The absence of trees, except for sparse bushes like birch and dwarf spruce, accentuates the dreary aspect of this granitic coast whose only adornments are moss and lichen.

21 Étang du Nord

As Cartier relates in the journal of his first voyage, on June 25, 1534, he discovered three islands at the northeastern tip of the Magdalen Islands. He named the largest one *Rocher aux Margaux ou des Oiseaux* (Magpie Rock). He was unable to land there since the island is a huge rock rising straight out of the sea to an altitude of 114 feet.

A more hospitable island can be seen five miles to the west. Cartier went there on June 26 and spent the night. This magnificent island two miles long, with sandy beaches, good arable land and tall trees, enchanted Cartier so much that he named it Brion after the French admiral who had commissioned him.

The next day, Cartier set off to explore land he had seen through the fog, about 10 miles to the west. He thought it was the mainland but it was the Magdalen Islands archipelago. Four miles from Brion Island, Cartier saw an impressive cape which he named "Cap Daulphin" (North Cape). Strong head winds prevented him from landing.

Near Old Harry Island, Cartier saw walrus seals frolicking on sand bars. He then sailed around the marshes on the northwest shores of Île au Loup and followed the land for about 10 miles.

J. Camille Pouliot
La grande aventure de Jacques Cartier

22 Cap au Trou

At the centre of the enclosed sea named Gulf of St. Lawrence, the Magdalen Island (Îles-de-la-Madeleine) look like a fishhook 97 kilometres long. The archipelago comprises fifteen islands and islets at various distances from one another, linked together by sand dunes or by underwater reefs.

23 L'Étang-du-Nord

Here, the gulf appears to be endless. It is always a great surprise for the traveller to discover that what looked like a dark spot spread out on the horizon is an archipelago. As the ship moves closer, the round or elongated shapes of the islands stand out. They still appear unrelated to one another, but, slowly, the outline of the dunes becomes clearer.

24 Île aux Goélands

Seagull Island (L'île aux Goélands) is a short distance from the west coast of Cap-aux-Meules island. It is one of the numerous islands that surround the archipelago, like so many outposts standing against a sea of many moods.

25 Île du Havre Aubert

The meeting of the two currents and the shallow depth of the water combined with strong eastern winds create a rough sea with rollers and breakers. Along with Sable Island, the archipelago deserves its sad reputation as "the cemetery of the Atlantic".

26 Île d'Entrée

Entrance Island (Île d'Entrée) is the highest island and the the only one detached from the archipelago. On the east shore its red cliffs stand 100 metres high. The village of Île d'Entrée, in the west, looks out on the larger islands.

27 Rocher aux Oiseaux

Petrels, puffins, murres, gannetts, gulls populate these two enormous rocks flanked with sheer cliffs where these aquatic birds have lived since 1919, sheltered from the "egg robbers" who used to haunt these inhospitable shores.

28 Refuge du Rocher-aux-Oiseaux

The cliffs bordering the Gulf of St. Lawrence, such as those of the Rocher-aux-Oiseaux, provide a refuge for the various species of aquatic birds, facilitating fishing. According to each species' behavior, the birds occupy different levels of the cliff: the gulls and the petrels usually live at the top, while black guillemots, for example, live in the rocks at the bottom of the cliff.

29 Île de Havre aux Maisons

On a clear day, this part of the gulf projects a unique mix of vivid colors — red cliffs, yellow sand and several shades of green vegetation and blue water. In bad weather, this island still has an unusual appearance. Isolated hills and sheer rock walls can be glimpsed through the rain and fog, linked by lines of surf that mask the sand bars.

Instructions nautiques
Golfe et fleuve Saint-Laurent

30 Île du Havre aux Maisons

Gypsum and sandstone, either grey-green or red, color the shores transformed by erosion into arches or tunnels.

31 La Vernière

In 1755, many Acadian families, fleeing persecution, left Prince Edward Island and Cape Breton for the Magdalen Islands. But the first attempt at colonization was not successful. As a matter of fact, in 1793, most of the population left the Magdalen Islands to settle on Cape Breton Island. However, the same year, several families from Miquelon Island, also of Acadian descent, driven out by the French Revolution, came to the Magdalens under the guidance of Father Jean-Baptiste Allain. They stayed and founded families. According to Senator Poirier, it is probably in the Magdalen Islands that the Acadian type is best preserved: strapping young men with great vitality and moral strength. It is rare to see people as happy with their lot, as attached to their soil, their rocks, their fishing.

Damase Potvin
Le Saint-Laurent et ses îles

32 Îles de la Madeleine

The ice obstructing the Gulf of St. Lawrence, off the archipelago, the sea ice of local origin, the estuary ice and, even, under certain circumstances, the ice in the vicinity of Labrador, welcomes home year after year various species of seals, especially the Greenland seal. At the end of a long migration they come to give birth to their young or to mate again.

33 Île du Havre aux Maisons

A typical house on the Magdalen Islands is Acadian in style, and usually painted in lively colors. Facing the sea, the houses were built along the road in a pattern which at first sight may seem anarchic, but depends, above all, on the whims of topography.

34 **Anse de l'Étang du Nord**
There lieth a wreck on the dismal shore
Of cole and pitiless Labrador;
Where, under the moon, upon mounts of frost,
Full many a mariner's bones are tost!

You shadowy bark hath been to that wreck,
And the dim blue fire, that lights her deck,
Doth play on as pale and livid a crew
As ever yet drank the church-yard dew!
Thomas Moore

35 **Prince Edward Island**
The tides, currents, winds and ice from the Gulf of St. Lawrence mold the coastline which is made of drifting dunes, creating some of the most beautiful beaches in North America.

36 **Cap Orby**
On the north shore of Prince Edward Island, the wind blowing from the gulf attacks the dunes which resist, thanks to the sand grass that protects them. First link of a long chain, the sand grass has roots three metres deep. This enables many plants and bushes to root along the shore and take various shapes, according to the currents and the wind.

37 **Baie des Chaleurs**
The shores of Baie des Chaleurs present a sharp contrast. The north shore is "a mountainous high land," while the south shore "is as beautiful and good an arable land and as beautiful a country, full of meadows, as we could ever see."

38 **Île de Pokeshaw**
The Island of Pokeshaw, a desolate rock off the coast of New Brunswick, in the Baie des Chaleurs, used to be part of the mainland.

39 **Aster**
Eastern North America is the favorite home of asters, and probably their birthplace.
Plantes sauvages des villes et des champs

40 **Cavendish**
Near Cavendish, in Prince Edward Island National Park, the erosion of the sandstone cliffs gives the beaches a reddish color, characteristic of the island.

41 Baie Mal Baie

Camille Pouliot writes that, according to a theory proposed by eminent geologists, "If Percé Rock was originally linked to the mainland and if this held true in 1534, we can easily understand why Cartier sailed two days in a row to the eastern side of the rock to seek shelter from head winds that often prevail between Cap d'espoir, Cap Blanc and Cap Enragé."

42 Cap du Nord

The northern part of Cape Breton Island overlooks the rugged coastline of the Gulf of St. Lawrence. Some granitic peaks reaching more than 400 metres above sea level bear witness to the tectonic activity that shaped these lands.

43 Anticosti Island

Archaeological excavations in the periphery of Anticosti Island, "Notiskuan" in the Amerindian language, revealed a human presence about 3,500 years ago. It appears that the first occupants left this ara, but kept coming back to it occasionally. Basque fishermen visited these shores before the arrival of the French explorers.

44 Pointe des Monts

For some authors like Raoul Blanchard the St.Lawrence estuary stops at Pointe des Monts, and for oceanographic and biological reasons P. Brunel solves the problem differently. L.E. Hamelin saw the limit between the estuary and the gulf in soutwest/norwest zone, cutting in half the Honguedo and Jacques Cartier straits, as well as Anticosti Island.

Jean-Claude Lasserre
Le Saint-Laurent

45 Rivière Jupiter

In the area of the Jupiter River, as on most of Anticosti Island, basalm fir, white spruce and black spruce predominate. But, in the eastern part groves become rarer and more scattered to make room for peat bogs, devoid of all trees.

46 Quatre-Temps

In the Abénaquis language, the name for the Four Seasons plant means "when one feels a stitch" because it is used to cure that kind of pain. It is a remedy for colds for the Manouan Indians who boil this plant with tea leaves from the woods. When boiled with hemlock twigs, it relieves painful menstruation.

Gisèle Lamoureux
Plantes sauvages printanières

47 Baie Sainte-Claire

Following his first voyage of discovery, Georges Martin-Zédé, governor of the island from 1896 to 1926, describing some of the mammals he found there, wrote in his journal: "Black bears exhibiting the characteristics of black, white and grizzly bears; red, silver or cross-breed foxes; martens whose tails are white at the tip; otters, near the source of rivers are all found on Anticosti Island."

Georges Martin-Zédé
Journal

48 Lac Geneviève

Henri Meunier, who bought Anticosti Island in 1895 for $125,000, brought over 200 deer from Virginia and about 20 moose to the island. The deer population has increased tremendously: it is now estimated at about 60,000.

49 Baie-Trinité

From the Saguenay River junction the scenery changes again. Receiving waters from this fjord that carved an enormous gap 200 metres long below the surface, the St. Lawrence River deepens suddenly to 300 metres and is 60 kilometres wide to the right of Baie-Comeau. The other shore is now barely visible.
Jean-Claude Lasserre
Le Saint-Laurent

50 Equisetum

There are about 25 species of these plants, called horsetails. They are the last and unique survivors of a category of flora that reached their fullest development at the end of the Stone Age, when they grew as tall as 30 metres.

51 Île du Havre aux Maisons

The main group of islands is connected in spots by sand bars rising barely one metre above the water, and in other spots by soaring dunes.

52 Rivière-Pentecôte

The places where major rivers flow into the sea have often developed into big cities or heavily-populated areas. In North America, the four rivers apart from the St. Lawrence that have had an important geographic role are all associated with big cities — the Hudson and New York, the Mississipi and New Orleans, the Columbia and Portland, the Fraser and Vancouver. But the St. Lawrence empties into a sparsely-populated region and a gulf bordered by particularly uninhabited shores.
Jean-Claude Lasserre
Le Saint-Laurent

53 Baie Martin

It is very difficult to tell how long ago Anticosti Island appeared in the Gulf of St. Lawrence. Data indicate that it emerged before the glacier period, two million years ago... After the continental ice shelf melted away, sea water submerged the area, then receded leaving the island surrounded with several layers of gravel.

> Allen Petryk
> *Report to the Department*
> *of Energy and Resources*

54 Rivière aux Saumons

About 100 rivers break up the landscape on Anticosti Island, the two biggest being the Jupiter and the Saumons. Most valleys include deep canyons where the peaceful streams turn into rapids and falls. At one point, the falls in the Rivière aux Saumons are 76 metres high.

55 Rivière-au-Tonnerre

There are three main kinds of lichen. Some cover rocks like crusts, some grow like shells in round patches and others spring up like tiny bushes with straight or drooping branches.

56 Mingan Islands

The Mingan Archipelago near Havre-Saint-Pierre numbers 23 islands and a dozen islets. These islands are made up of several layers of limestone, sloping slightly to the south. About 60 million years ago, rivers burrowed between the flower pot rocks that are now battered by the sea on the northern shores of the islands, while leaving vast lowlands on the southern shores.

57 Île à Firmin

The Mingan Islands feature evolving high cliffs rising out of still waters, ancient beaches, surfaces smoothed out by the sea and monolith rocks shaped by erosion, known as "flower pots" or "stout women."

58 Nid de Corbeau

Although land mammals are numerous on Anticosti Island, there may be an even greater quantity of fish and sea mammals. Herds of seals come to rest on the island at certain times of the year. Close to shore one can find capelin, mackerel, herring and halibut. Lobsters and crabs are plentiful on the continental shelf. On the other hand, there is no commercial fishing on a large scale.

59 Île du Fantôme
The immense flat surfaces, cliffs, lakes and biotopes such as sandy moors, salt marshes, peat bogs, as well as the sea, offer ideal habitat for numerous species of aquatic birds. The flora is equally varied: over 500 plants, several of which are typical of the islands, and about 100 mosses and lichens. The Mingan archipelago is covered with forests; evergreens, mostly balsam fir, cover most of the islands.

60 Rivière Moisie
The Moisie River flows into the gulf on the east side of Moisie Point, between sandy banks. The river carries sand during the spring floods; this sand forms sandbars rolling down one kilometre from the mouth of the river.

Instructions nautiques
Golfe et fleuve Saint-Laurent

61 Marguerite
The huge, varied daisy family includes 25,000 varieties. Their buds often have silky crowns and they spread widely through wind dispersion.

62 Chou puant
In the early spring, the heat inside the shoot can melt the snow around it. All parts of the plant give off a smell of decay when broken. In the fall, one can often see a shiny horn-shaped bud that will bloom in the spring.

Gisèle Lamoureux
Plantes sauvages printanières

63 Petit prêcheur
In the St. Lawrence River lowlands and in certain areas of the Laurentian and Appalachian Mountains, these small birds are common in damp woods along streams.

64 Rivière Sainte-Marguerite
While the soil in northern forests is very moist, the trees absorb very little water because the earth remains frozen for the better part of the year. Evergreens are particularly well adapted to this dryness but only a few species—fir, pine and spruce—are found. They all have very thick needles that prevent water loss through evaporation.

Le monde étrange et
fascinant des animaux

65 Port Cartier
In the early fifties, shipping traffic rose considerably in the St. Lawrence as iron ore ports were developed to handle shipments from new mines in Northern Québec and Labrador with rich deposits. Shipments of iron ore have been the main activity in the ports of Port Cartier, Sept-Îles and Pointe-Noire.

66 Rivière aux Outardes
Water from the Outardes River contains floating bits of white soil and is lighter than salt water. It often covers the whole Baie aux Outardes, making it look shallow. A ship sailing in this fresh water leaves a blue wake.

67 Baie des Sept-Îles
Sept-Îles' Seaway offers a deep water area, about 5 kilometres wide. The bottom is made of clay and the Seaway is free of shoals.

68 Sept-Îles
Although Sept-Îles is the chief town in this area it was founded recently, like all the hamlets on the Coast. Seventy-five years ago there were only two or three shanties occupied by families of fishermen.
Damase Potvin,
Le Saint-Laurent et ses îles.

69 Baie Sainte-Marguerite
Although fish is plentiful near the estuary banks, coastal fishery shows a sharp decline, whereas deep-sea fishing is on the increase. Pollution of the river may, to some extent, discourage fishing in this area.

70 Monts Chic-Chocs
Parc de la Gaspésie covers a vast, rugged area of deep valleys and peaks nearly 1,200 metres high. The Chic-Chocs Mountains belong to the Appalachian mountain range and constitute their backbone. The tallest ones are the McGerrigle Mountains.

71 Mont Sainte-Anne
St. Anne Mountain, which overlooks the town of Percé, reaches an altitude of 375 metres.

72 Baie Mal Baie
The south shore of Mal Baie Bay, between Percé Rock and Cannes-de-Roches, is lined with steep cliffs nearly 200 metres high.

73 Pic de l'Aurore
From the top of Pic de l'Aurore, one of the many cliffs lining up the Gaspesian coast, one discovers Bonaventure island, the Percé Rock and, in the distance, the Baie des Chaleurs.

74 Pic de l'Aurore
On one side the unbounded sea, and on the other an incomparable scenery: Les trois soeurs, Mont-Sainte-Anne (Champlain named it the "table à Rolante") and the majestic Pic de l'Aurore.

> J. Camille Pouliot
> *La grande aventure de Jacques Cartier*

75 Presqu'île Forillon
Except for a few coastal areas, Forillon National Park covers most of the small Forillon Peninsula. Its name comes from *pharillon* (small lighthouse). In Champlain's days, this name was given to a cliff 270 metres high, facing Gaspé Cape, and on which fires were lit to warn fishing boats of danger.

76 Cap Gaspé
This rock is of marine origin. The proof is that several layers of marine deposits are clearly visible on the cliffs and rocks. These layers — slanted, wrinkled and sometimes turned upside down — bear witness to the gigantic forces that molded the landscape in the earliest times.

77 Gaspé Bay
Gaspé Bay covers 23 kilometres of coastline and features a sheltered harbour and an excellent outer mooring area.

78 Cap Bon-Ami
Gaspé Peninsula's coves and capes were generally named after the sailors who were shipwrecked or stayed in the area. This is why *Cap-aux-Os* should read *Cap "Ozo"*, for the first man from Guernsey who lived there. *Anse-à-la-Rogne*, between Grand-Étang and Cloridorme, derives its name from and old fisherman named Milliard. One kilometre above is Anse-à-Breton, named after a Breton shipwecked in that area. We also have *Anse-à-Vallée, Anse-à-Paradis*, above Cloridorme, *Anse-à-Fisher* the *Arbour river, Pointe-à-Lamonde, Cape "Bon Amy"*, below Cap-Rosier... all these are fishermen's names. Toward Rimouski, in St.Thomas and other places, several families are called Desrosiers. I am enclined to believe that a sailor or fisherman with this name was either shipwrecked there of lived in the Cape area. In this case, one should write "Cap Desrosiers". This is my opinion, but everyone has a right to its own.

> Letter from M. Bossé, missionary at
> Cap-des-Rosiers, to Mgr. Cayeau.

79 Île Bonaventure
In the old days, there was a small fishing village on Bonaventure Island. Since 1919, however, the island has been a refuge for many species of aquatic birds such as gannetts, cormorans, gulls and petrels. The island's gannett colony, estimated at 50,000 birds, is the largest and most accessible of the 22 gannett colonies around the world.

80 Rivière de l'Anse-au-Griffon
Forillon National Park offers a wide variety of unusual plant life, especially on the Penouille dunes and in the Penouille Bay saltwater marshes. In addition to these particularly interesting spots, many kinds of vegetation can be seen — hardwood stands, evergreen stands, mixed woods, dune plants, meadows, freshwater marshes and salt marshes.

81 Cap Bon-Ami
Between Cap Gaspé and Cap Bon-Ami, steep limestone cliffs soar 200 metres above sea level. In this part of the peninsula, the coastline bears traces of ancient marine terraces, stacked up as evidence of repeated drops in the sea level.

82 Cap Bon-Ami
A unique mountain flora is found on the east coast of the peninsula at Cap Bon-Ami. Botanists do not know why this type of Arctic or Alpine perennial vegetation has survived. It may date back to the glacier period.

83 Mont Saint-Alban
Saint-Alban Mountain rises straight above the cliffs that border the eastern side of the Forillon peninsula, near Cap Bon-Ami.

84 Baie de Gaspé
The Micmac Indians used to inhabit the territory that is now the Maritimes. In the XVth century, pressured by the White man, many Micmacs went up north to New Brunswick and Gaspé (...) The Micmacs belong to the eastern Algonquins group and have several of the characteristics found in the Algonquins from Central Canada, especially the Objiways.

85 Grande-Grève
Forillon National Park covers a narrow peninsula, bordered to the south by Gaspé Bay and jutting out into the Gulf of St. Lawrence. For thousands of years, the crashing waves and other forms of erosion have carved the park's coastline into fascinating shapes.

86 Caplan
Some say this village on the Baie des Chaleurs was named after a Micmac, John Caplan, who lived there when white settlers arrived. Others say the name comes from capelin, a small fish of the salmon type.

87 Rivière-au-Tonnerre

In the Gulf of St. Lawrence, the currents result from the horizontal movements of the waters influenced by tides, winds and atmospheric pressure. The direction of the currents varies according to the flow and ebb, but they can be slowed down, reversed or intensified when all these factors meet. In the free waters of the Gulf the currents' speed rarely exceeds one knot; consequently, their direction is strongly influenced by meteorologic conditions. To sum up, the Gulf's currents run counterclockwise.

Instructions nautiques,
Golfe et fleuve Saint-Laurent.

88 Rivière-à-Claude

The small village of Rivière-à-Claude does not differ much from the other towns along the Gaspé coast, except that its name is in dispute. Some historians argue that it was originally called Rivière-à-Claude after the local name for gulls.

89 Parc de la Gaspésie

Parc de la Gaspésie, a provincial park, is one of the few places in Québec where caribou, moose and deer roam the same territory. The caribou, facing extinction in this region, can be found on the McGerrigle, Albert and Jacques Cartier mountains.

90 Bic

Bic harbour is deep and safe. In 1759, the British fleet carrying General Wolfe's army stopped here. For a long time, Bic was a naval outpost.

91 Bic

During the French Regime, wrote J.-Edouard Roy, ships entering the river made for Bic Island, then veered off toward Tadoussac. This means that the island played an important role in our history, especially during the French Regime... Missionaries who navigated this part of the river with the Indians in their bark canoes made the island a rallying point.

Damase Potvin
Le Saint-Laurent et ses îles

92 Bic

Bic is mentioned in *The History of Emily Montagne,* the first Canadian novel, published in London in 1767 by the wife of Francis Brooke, chaplain of the British troops.

93 Baie de Gaspé

"*Gaspeg* is a Micmac word that means 'promontory.' Even before the Micmacs moved into this region, the name Gaspé had replaced 'Honguedo', as this region was called once. Gaspé is mentioned for the first time by Haklyut."

J.-Camille Pouliot
La Grande aventure de Jacques Cartier

94 Rivière-Pigou

Fish is abundant in the St. Lawrence River. Its grey and green waters make a marvellous fish-pond; they supply marine life with carbon dioxide, necessary to planton, and with oxygen and all kinds of mineral salts. Greater quantities of salt dissolve more easily, but are heavier and tend to slide to the bottom. Fortunately, rain, water from rivers and melting icebergs replenish the surface waters with salt. In certain privileged areas, cold waters bring their mineral salts to the surface. This explains the Gulf's unusual colours.

Bernard Boivin
Le monde de Jacques Cartier

95 Kamouraska

Local fishermen use small boats and weirs that catch the attention of visitors, standing out in the landscape of the estuary. These wooden weirs lead to enclosures where the fish are trapped. In this way, large quantities of eels, sturgeons and herrings are caught, usually picked up with a tractor at low tide.

Jean-Claude Lasserre
Le Saint-Laurent

96 Mont-Saint-Pierre

After entering the Gulf of St. Lawrence, the Atlantic tides roll up the river all the way to Lake Saint-Pierre near Montréal, 640 kilometres upstream from Sept-Îles. Twice a day, high tide takes about one hour to travel from Sept-Îles to the mouth of the Saguenay River, five hours to reach Québec City and ten hours to get to Lake Saint-Pierre.

97 Saint-Roch-des-Aulnaies

The north shore of the St. Lawrence Valley is made up of hills and an almost continuous plateau 300 metres high, stretching from the Ottawa River to the Strait of Belle Isle. The only major break occurs at the wide mouth of the Saguenay River. The south shore has the same appearance from Gaspé to Sainte-Anne-des-Monts. Upstream, however, the mountains fade into the distance, leaving room for a strip of lowlands.

98   Île aux Grues

Why the name Île aux Grues? Because wandering cranes called by Horace—*gruen advenam*—returning from Florida during the great spring migration down the St. Lawrence found on this hospitable island a refuge for rest, feeding and breeding.

Damase Potvin
Le Saint-Laurent et ses îles

99   Cap à l'Orignal

A stream originating at Lake Vaseux flows into a cove between Cap à l'Orignal and the rivershore near Bic. The area around the lake offers the first glimpse of the unusual Bic mountain ranges — narrow ridges of grey rock parallel to the coast, separated by deep valleys.

100   Charlevoix

Successive glacier movements have gouged, buckled and heaved up the Charlevoix landscape. These movements left impressive cliffs near Saint-Siméon known as the *palissades*, and moraine deposits at Lake Nairn, near Clermont.

101   Île aux Coudres

James Cook is a national hero in Britain, Australia and New Zealand. Few people know that he demonstrated his remarkable talents for hydrography and scientific exploration in Québec. It is to this self-taught Captain, considered the greatest explorer of his day, that we owe the first reliable charts of the St. Lawrence River and estuary.

102   Baie-Saint-Paul

In the earliest days of New France, Baie Saint-Paul became a stopping-off point for captains sailing up the St. Lawrence, probably because the wide and deep valley foud here is a rare inviting spot along the north shore.

103   Île aux Oies

At low tide, the sandbar linking Île aux Oies with Île aux Grues emerges from the river. A large quantity of coarse hay is harvested here and shipped to Québec City and to villages on both sides of the St. Lawrence.

104   Saint-Irénée

In the hamlet of Saint-Irénée we find the house that once belonged to Adolphe Routhier, who wrote the lyrics of *Ô Canada*, the national anthem. The village was built close to what the residents call the sea. Every year in late April or early May, thousands of capelins swarm ashore.

105 Saguenay River

The Saguenay River looks like a long and narrow mountain lake. The river, half a mile wide in spots and two miles wide in others, flows into the St. Lawrence at right angles, between tall mountains of syenitic granite and gneiss. Everywhere, the mountains rise above the river in more or less sheer cliffs, some of them more than 300 metres high. These peaks, lined up over a great distance along this magnificent river, offer a wild, barren and scenic view. The granite hills are mostly bare, but the valleys shelter swift streams flowing over deep layers of sand and clay. For the first 50 miles upstream, the Saguenay is nearly as deep as the mountains are tall. Along most of the length of the river, from Pointe Noire to Baie des Ha! Ha!, water depth varies from 180 to 272 metres.

Instructions nautiques
Golfe et fleuve Saint-Laurent

106 Sainte-Rose-du-Nord

The village of Sainte-Rose-du-Nord formerly was known as La Descente-des-Femmes. According to Arthur Buies, this name recalled an adventure experienced by Indian women who were sent by their husbands to get help and who came upon the Saguenay in En Bas Cove after walking for a long time along a small stream.

107 Saguenay River

The Saguenay River is the only tributary of the St. Lawrence deep enough for navigation. It leads to two ports serving a farming area in the heart of Québec's northern forests and a relatively isolated lake region known as the "kingdom of the Saguenay". At the northern end of a true fjord nearly 100 kilometres long, on the shores of the vast and deep Baie des Ha! Ha!, you find the wharves of Port-Alfred, and a short distance to the west on the right bank, those of Chicoutimi.

Jean-Claude Lasserre
Le Saint-Laurent

108 Sabot de la Vierge

Lady's slippers belong to the orchid family. They are perennials. They grow across the province of Quebec, all the way up to James Bay and, in the east, as far as Natashquan.

109 Monotropa Uniflora

This white plant with tinges of pink does not contain clorophyl. It grows in bunches and is called saprophytic, meaning that it feeds on decaying organic matter.

110 Cap Tourmente

For six weeks each spring and fall, more than 100,000 snow geese stop at Cap Tourmente on their migrations between Baffin Island and the Caribbean, where they winter. Other bird species such as mallards flock to the sandbanks of Cap Tourmente, where they feed in the rushes.

111 Île d'Orléans

Village of St. Jean was built near the Maheu River, named after René Maheu who as early as 1651 owned the river banks. He was also the first sea captain to reside in St. Jean, and apparently started a tradition since the parish has always numbered a great many sea captains and sailors. The importance of this group, as well as prosperous farmers and numerous vacationers, made St. Jean the "capital" until the inauguration of the bridge.

112 Saint-François

The parish of Saint-François is rather different from all the other parishes on the island. It belongs to the great spaces: located on the east of the island, the village is very small because its population —mostly farmers— is scattered on the land.

113 Les Éboulements

Nous apprenons du costé de Tadoussac, que l'effort du Tremble-terre n'y a pas esté moins rude qu'ailleurs; qu'on y a veu une pluye de cendre, qui traversoit le fleuve comme auroit fait un gros orage, et que, qui voudroit suivre toute la coste depuis le Cap de Tourmente jusques-là, verroit des effets prodigieux. Vers la Baye dite de S. Paul, il y avoit une petite montagne sise sur le bord du fleuve, d'un quart de lieuë ou environ de tour, laquelle s'est abysmée, et comme elle n'eust fait que plonger, elle est ressortie du fond de l'eau pour se changer en islette, et faire d'un lieu tout bordé d'écueils, comme il estoit, un havre d'asseurauce contre toutes sortes de vents.

Jérôme Lalemant

114 Pain de sucre

During the cold season, fine and tiny drops of water from the Montmorency Falls freeze and in landing form a giant cone which can reach a height of over 25 metres, called "pain de sucre" (sugar cone) by the residents of the region. This natural structure is used for tobogganing.

115 Chute Montmorency

Montmorency Falls, 83 metres high, are the result of geological upheavals millions years ago and of a rapid erosion that took place in the Quarternary Period.

116 Charny

At the top of the waterfalls situated in Charny, there used to be a mission and an Abenaquis cemetery. The Falls inspired Champlain, in 1633, to call the river "noisy river".

117   Chute de la Chaudière
The Chaudière River spills over at Charny, slightly upstream of its mouth, hollowed by a basin resembling a boiler.

118   Québec
As it progresses northeast, the St. Lawrence flows into a gorge. Downstream of Dracona its width lessens, while the shores are surmounted by slopes higher and higher and more and more abrupt. Hence, at the end of this evolution, the extraordinary "breakthrough" of Québec where the river, only one kilometre wide flows majestically between two cliffs "about a hundred metres high".

> Jean-Claude Lasserre,
> *Le Saint-Laurent.*

119   Lévis
Built face to face, the cities of Québec and Lévis overlook the strait that gave Québec its name — so it is said. In the Amerindian language, Québec means narrowing.

Lauzon and Lévis are adjacent and one goes from one to the other without noticing it. If Lévis witnessed the birth of commander Alphonse Desjardins, founder of the "Caisses Populaires", Lauzon possesses important Shipyards. Champlain's dry dock is 350 metres long.

120   Bassin Louise
Although Québec's harbour is open year round, the ships sailing up to Québec must nevertheless be strengthened against the ice, from January to March inclusive.

121   Québec
Between Québec and Lake Saint-Pierre, drifting ice flows continuously toward the sea with occasional obstructions, especially ahead of the Québec bridge where the river is considerably narrower. At Carnaval time, the St. Lawrence, cluttered with ice, becomes the site of a boat race that commemorates the crossings of yerteryear.

122   Place Royale
Cradle of the French occupation of the St. Lawrence Valley, Place Royale is erected on the very site of Champlain's "Habitation".

123   Québec
If, after numerous unsuccessful attempts on the American continent, France finally settled on the St. Lawrence, it is due for the most part to one man's action, Champlain, who succeeded in convincing the Sieur de Monts, lieutenant general of New France and holder of a monopoly on trade in the great St. Lawrence River...

> Jean-Claude Lasserre,
> *Le Saint-Laurent.*

124 Rivière Chaudière

Between Québec city and Trois-Rivières, the rocky and high coast line of the St. Lawrence estuary gives place to the lightly wooded and comparatively lowlands of lower St. Lawrence, lands of intensive farming.

125 Pointe des Monts

It is often foggy in the lower part of the river during the summer months because of the relative coolness of the water surface. With the hot and humid airflow from the southwest this effect is accentuated and the fog becomes thicker and more persistant. Even moderate winds cannot disperse this kind of fog. Above Québec city, in the Fall, the fog is more likely to produce sand-banks along the river, early in the morning, in nice weather or gentle winds.

> *Instructions nautiques,*
> *Golfe et fleuve Saint-Laurent.*

126 Saint-Étienne-de-Beaumont

From Saint-Étienne-de-Beaumont, one automatically looks at the south shore of Orleans Island (l'Île d'Orléans). The present church was built in 1733. It is on that church's door that Wolfe had his 1759 proclamation posted. The villagers tore it immediately and the soldiers set the church on fire by way of reprisals, but only the door burned down.

127 Les Becquets

In temperate forests, evergreens are becoming progressively rarer; they are replaced by hardwood, as in the region of Lake Saint-Pierre. The winter is shorter than in the regions where the boreal forest predominates, but cold enough to stop the process of photosynthesis process. The trees take a momentary rest ofter losing their leaves which are sensitive to frost.

128 Trois-Rivières

Trois-Rivières was the first Canadian locality to own a heavy industry, the famous Forges du Saint-Maurice, created in 1729. They were the first to make birch canoes 12 metres long, called *rabaskas*, distortion of Arthabasca, name of a river in the Canadian west which was borrowed, along with the boats, by the fur merchants and the voyageurs in the last century.

129 Berthierville

Berthierville is advantageously located on the north channel of the St. Lawrence River, at the mouth of the Bayonne River and at the west end of lake Saint-Pierre. This natural and shallow lake, used by the St. Lawrence seaway, is dredged at a depth of 10,668 metres (35 feet) so the St. Lawrence channel can be free.

130 Grandes-Piles

The village of Grandes-Piles is built on a cliff overlooking the Saint-Maurice, tributary of the St. Lawrence. Because the river is navigable upstream up to La Tuque, the village was a transhipment port in the XIXth century.

131 Cap-de-la-Madeleine

The town of Trois-Rivières is situated on the west coast of the mouth of Saint-Maurice River; Cap-de-la-Madeleine is on the other side, vis-à-vis Trois-Rivières. These two towns have numerous factories, including many paper pulp and paper mills. Through the seaway, Québec is 103 kilometres away and Montréal 113 kilometres.

132 Sorel

The port of Sorel located near the central area of the St. Lawrence is not known for its industry. Grain, ilmenite and anthracite represent the major imports. Other imports are pigiron, steel ingots, laminated steel rollers and... grain. In all: about ten million tonnes handled every year.

133 Saint-Lambert

Saint-Lambert locks mark the entrance to the St. Lawrence Seaway. Officially inaugurated June 26, 1959, this seaway enables ships, thanks to a canal with two locks, to pass through the Lachine Rapids and the Sainte-Marie's current; two other locks are located between the canal of Beauharnois' power station and lake Saint-Louis. A second canal, equally equipped with two locks makes it possible to circumvent, on American soil, the installations of Barnhart Island. The last lock is located at Iroquois, next to the water level control dam. For the remaining distance of 302 kilometres, the ships navigate in a channel.

134 Montréal

Montréal is the meeting point of the shipping channel and the St. Lawrence seaway. From this port ships can sail, about eight months of the year, as far as Duluth at the end of Lake Superior, a distance of 1,863 kilometres. In addition to three grain elevators with a combined capacity of 550,000 tonnes, the port of Montréal boasts varied equipment: at wharf 58, a bridge-crane for handling coal and bulk cargo; at wharf 71, two 27-tonnes cranes on wheels to unload oil and dry bulk cargo. The container terminal at gates 60-61 has cranes that can lift shipments of 35 and 40 tonnes, respectively. There is another container terminal, with roll-on roll-off facilities and a 35-tonne crane, at gate 66. Elsewhere, you can find two 45-tonne cranes and one 40-tonne crane on wheels.

135 Rapides de Lachine

At the beginning of the XVIIIth century, Dallier de Casson, Superior of the Sulpicians in Montreal, started building a 1,6 kilometre-long canal to circumvent the most dangerous part of the Lachine Rapids. This undertaking the first attempt to canalize the St. Lawrence River.

136 Montréal

The city is one of the most remarkable cross-roads of land and water transportation routes in North America. The city borders on a fertile plain with rich farmland and a milder climate than in neighbouring areas. Human settlement was bound to occur here at the foot of the first rapids in the river. Nature did its share by placing a volcanic mountain in the centre, surrounded by two superimposed sea beds left behind by the receding Champlain sea. This created a vast area where a city could develop close to water but well protected from flooding. Part of the lowlands were cut off from the rest of the island by a recent ravine, creating an easily fortified area near the shore. This are was an ideal place to start a settlement.

Raoul Blanchard,
L'Ouest du Canada français.

137 Montréal

The great island of Montréal, or Hochelaga archipelago, is formed by two rivers that meet: the St. Lawrence River and its tributary the Outaouais, which changes its name when it flows into Deux-Montagnes lake (...). This lake empties into the river on three sides: Sainte-Anne-de-Bellevue Rapids and Des Prairies and Mille-Îles rivers.

Damase Potvin,
Le Saint-Laurent et ses îles.

138 Boucherville

Near Boucherville, the 735-kilowatts electric power line across the St. Lawrence carries energy produced by the great rivers of the North Shore and Labrador.

139 Sorel

Metallurgical plants, machine shops, and electric furfurnaces give the town of Sorel a particular character as they also do to its close neighbours, Saint-Joseph-de-Sorel and Tracy. Most of these industries have access to harbour waters.

140 The Great Lakes

The formation of the Laurentian shield came relatively recently in history as the final accident in the slow retreat of the ice cap from North America. In the chronology defined by J.L. Hough, the last remnants of the sea disappeared from the Laurentians 6,000 years ago, and the Plains River that drained the north, 2,000 years ago. Thus it was only in this era that the Great Lakes began to flow exclusively into the St. Lawrence instead of the Mississipi.

Jean-Claude Lasserre,
Le Saint-Laurent.

Index

Mia and Klaus Matthes opened their studio in 1958. Since then they have been travelling to the four corners of the world in search of unfamiliar images.

A number of their photographs have been published in such periodicals as *Merian* in Germany, *Figaro Magazine* in France, *Perspectives* in Quebec, as well as in books published by the *Reader's Digest* and the National Film Board, such as *Between Friends, Canada du temps qui passe, Images, Canada*.

Bonjour Québec, the first book by Mia and Klaus, with 45 photographs and a text by the painter Alfred Pellan, was published by McClelland and Stewart (Toronto) in 1967. The large format volume was presented in a slipcase. In 1968, their second book, *Québec et l'Île d'Orléans*, with text by poet Gatien Lapointe, was published in Quebec by Les Éditions du Pélican. Les Éditions du Jour brought out *Le corps secret* in 1969, with text by poet and critic Jacques Brault. In 1976, *Musique d'été* appeared at Les Éditions Fides.

In the spring of 1980, Les Éditions Libre Expression published *Québec*, by Mia and Klaus, a volume containing 189 colour photographs with a poem entitled *Choregraphy of a country*, by Gatien Lapointe, and in 1983 *Montreal*, containing 151 colour photographs and a text dedicated to the city, signed by the writer François Barcelo.

Over the years, the photographs of Mia and Klaus have been shown in various parts of the world, as part of exhibitions organized by the National Film Board and the Canadian Department of External Affairs. In Quebec, they have been shown at Man and His World, Place des Arts, the Musée d'art contemporain (on China, one of many countries they have visited), and at the Bibliothèque Nationale. In the framework of activities commemorating the 450th anniversary of Jacques Cartier, an exhibit of Mia and Klaus' photographs is on display in Saint-Malo.

All photographs in this volume were taken with Leica
cameras and Leitz lenses:
Fisheye-Elmarit-R 1: 2,8/16 mm
Super-Angulon-R 1: 4/21 mm
Elmarit-R 1: 2,8/28 mm
Elmarit-R 1: 2,8/35 mm
Summicron-R 1: 2/50 mm
Summicron-R 1: 2/90 mm
Elmarit-R 1: 2,8/135 mm
Apo-Telyt-R 1: 3,4/180 mm
Telyt 1: 6,8/400 mm
Super-Elmar-R: f/3.5/15
Macro-Elmarit-R: f/2.8/60

The original edition "The St.Lawrence" contains 140 photographs in color. Production by Henri Rivard; graphic design by France Lafond. Typesetting, in Baskerville, by L'Enmieux. Color separation is by Adco Litho. The first printing, consisting of 7000 copies on Rolland Imperial 200M, was printed under the supervision of Henri Rivard on the presses of Boulanger Printer, in Montreal, on March twenty-one, nineteen hundred and eighty-four.